For the people who inspire my passion for living:
Gary, Blythe, and my new little Chance.
I love you forever.

Acknowledgments

Without the support of my good-humored husband, Gary, this book would have never been possible.

Thanks so much to my good friends and advisors Jean and Don, who inspired and encouraged me to eat as much chocolate naked as possible while finishing this big project. My agent and editor Gareth Esersky and Deb Werksman, thanks for believing in my voice.

Thank you Pam and Marty and Bette and Mickey for helping me to live out my dreams and providing that "village" that every parent needs. Stacey and Kendall, thanks so much for being there all these years.

Most of all, thank you Blythe, for teaching me what's most important in life.

Table of Contents

section one

rethinking romance

I.

Rethinking Love

f your flame has been burning on the low side for a while, chances are you need a little more romance in your life. Where did it run off to? There may have been a time in your life when you were better at romance, when it came easily to you, and it may feel like those days are gone.

They're still here. Romance didn't abandon *you*. Perhaps on a busy and extraordinarily hectic day, you unintentionally started drifting away from it—and kept on going. *Eat Chocolate Naked* is calling you back to romance, calling you back to the little things that add sparkle to your life and a reason to get up and greet each new day with anticipation and excitement.

Romance isn't just a prelude to sex. It isn't even something that must be created by or for your lover. Romance is that extra touch you add that awakens the senses, like rosemary sprigs and eucalyptus oil added to a bath you've drawn just for yourself. It can be a tea candle that you keep lit in the window until your child comes home from a late night out. It can be the fiery fun that actually *is* a prelude to sex. And it can be something completely indulgent but simple, something like *eating chocolate naked*. It can be all these things and more. It's what makes life special in very simple, very meaningful ways.

There was a time, not very long ago, in fact, when my flame was burning pretty low. Let's put it this way: if I had been a lighthouse, there would have been shipwrecks and barges running aground across miles of shore-line. It was burning *low*.

I recognized the problem and decided quite easily that it was my husband's fault and that *he* needed to fix it. It seemed so simple: I *used* to feel that romantic sparkle in my life, I *didn't* anymore—it couldn't be *my* fault, so it must be *his*! Unfortunately, Gary didn't buy into this perfectly obvious and logical way of assessing the problem. I was forced to look at it from other angles.

And here's what I came up with: it's up to you to make your life more romantic in the ways you want it to be. It's very possible to encourage men to help create *more* romantic moments in a woman's life, and they can even grow to greatly enjoy the little romantic things we like so much: moonlit walks, candlelight kisses, surprise gifts, carriage rides. But the simple, unfortunate fact is that when those romantic things drift away again, they just don't notice (or care about) their absence quite as much as we do.

Men, like my husband, may be genuinely better than most women at seeing romance in the steady rhythms of everyday family life. While I applaud that gift, I admit that I, like most women, have a greater need. *I need sparkle.* Not all the time—just often enough that I know that it's still there. Still a living part of my life. *Romance!*

Romance is an integral part of the female nature. We need it. To deny ourselves romance is to deny ourselves spiritual oxygen.

It's about expressing our femininity in a way that pleases *us*. Women are multifaceted. Romance is about expressing all those facets. One day, you're the temptress. Another, you're the Victorian lady, or the athletic queen, or the mystical stargazer.

Romance is about expressing all those romantic versions of you. It's about making your home reflect those qualities in you. And it's about going out and seeking things that further enliven all the aspects of romantic you.

Getting back to romance may require a little letting go. Don't stop him from buying the single red rose from the lady who peddles them from table to table. Who cares if he spends too much for it?

Getting back to romance may also require some patience and some gentle instruction aimed at your man. Many surveys (not surprisingly, many conducted for the floral industry) find that women—almost *all* of us—consider romance critically important in a relationship. But here's the surprising news: the same percentage of men (91 percent in one survey) feel exactly the same way. Men want more romance, too. But many of them don't know how to make it happen. We can gently, romantically, teach them what we want.

But the biggest challenge may be inside yourself. It may be so long ago that you felt a true connection with your romantic nature that you've forgotten what you would even ask for if your mate offered to make three romantic wishes come true. *We have to remember what romance is.*

This book is about helping you make that connection once again. It's about creative ideas that will help you find your passions and build a better relationship with the romantic side of yourself. Some of the ideas offered, like giving romantic gifts, are things that you've done many times before.

Other ideas, like renting a single-wide trailer or Naked Bill Night are probably things you'd never, ever think of. Many ideas, like catnapping before romance, are based in the science of recent discoveries between men and women and brain chemicals that make us want romance more. Try them and have fun with them. Don't take anything, even romance, too seriously.

I hope you find yourself inspired to explore and reconnect romantically with your partner, and with all the romance just waiting for permission to *Eat Chocolate Naked*.

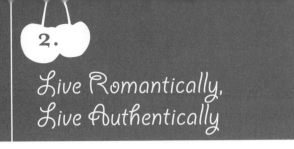

2.
Live Romantically, Live Authentically

Have you ever had a slow revelation about something? A revelation that doesn't konk you over the head all at once, but takes years to sink in and take over, and when it does you never look at anything the same way again? That's the kind of revelation I've experienced on the subject of women and romance.

The revelation began years before I actually sat down to write this book. I started out thinking that romance was a problem that women had with men. If we could only get men to understand our needs for romance and how to give it to us, our problems would be solved. But now I realize that men aren't the problem. We are.

Many of us are walking around starving for something, only we don't know what that something is. It's called authenticity. We are, in fact, starving for ourselves. We want to be more real, more us, more authentic in our daily lives in expressing who we really are. And many of us are, at heart, romantics.

Many of us, for innumerable reasons, have shut out part of ourselves. The side that yearns for romance, femininity, mystery, power, and vulnerability all wrapped up into one.

We've shut out the romance of living as a woman. We no longer celebrate womanhood, perhaps the way we once did when we were girls just trying out our woman-wings for the first time.

Living more romantically, then, for many of us, automatically means living more authentically. It means living life as you would if you were to, every day, live from the heart. If every day really meant something special, you would automatically live more romantically and authentically.

You would wear something that made you feel treasured. You would nurture yourself and others as if that day meant something special. You would nourish your body the way you would on a special occasion. You would love fully and mark the day with special rituals like lighting a candle, playing some music, or taking time to look at the stars.

Living more romantically doesn't mean doing a hundred things in one day that fit the authentic you. You could do just *one* small thing and start to feel that sense of starvation fade away. You would already be living 100 percent more authentically.

When it comes right down to it, getting men to participate in our needs for romance accounts for only a small part of the romantic authenticity we're yearning for. The rest can only be done by us. When we're starving for *us*, a generous helping of someone else's kindness is wonderful but doesn't do much to ease the hunger pains.

If you start living your life more romantically authentic, you're going to feel your life change in a dramatic way, even though the changes in things you do might seem tiny and insignificant. You will radiate love. Your lover will feel the difference and want to be a part of the change. Your family will feel the difference, and the love will grow branches.

Think about what living authentically means to you. Think about what romance in your life would look like if it were something you alone created every day, just for the sake of being more authentically you. Would you light more candles at home? Would you spend a few minutes each day reading poetry, something you love but haven't done for years? Would you keep fresh flowers in your house all the time?

The answer to romantic authenticity is in your heart, and it may be what you're looking for, starving for. Spend some time soul-searching to discover what it would take for your life on the *outside* to better reflect what your romantic nature is on the *inside*. What would your perfect day, your perfect life look like? How would it make you feel inside? How can you create that feeling, even for just a moment, every single day? Once you open the door to dreams perhaps long forgotten, you'll likely be flooded with ideas for how to make your life more romantic and more authentic.

3.
Map Your Way to the Mood

*"A poem, a sentence, causes us to see ourselves.
I be, and I see my being, at the same time."*
—Ralph Waldo Emerson

*P*ick up a pen and start writing in a journal. Write about any-thing. Let the words flow out of you and onto the page effort-lessly. Write about what you're feeling and what your daydreams are like.

Take it a step further and write about what a perfect day would look like—from sunrise to sunset—through your eyes. Would it start *before* dawn, with two cups of coffee, your lover, and the first twinges of orange color rising in the east, signaling the calling to a new day? How would your perfect day continue? How would it end?

If this exercise has you stumped, not because of a struggle for the right words, but because you just can't think of *anything* romantic you'd like to do in your perfect day, that's a signal to you that journaling, meditating, and spending more time with your thoughts is a must. You need to get to know yourself again, romantic side and all.

Journaling is the cheapest form of effective therapy you can get, and no one will interrupt you mid-sentence to inform you that your hour is up. Journals don't have to be boring logs of what you did on any given day. The new age of journaling is about writing down anything and everything that comes to mind.

In your journal, you're free to be as wild and silly as you like. If you've had a particularly boring day, write a fun, fictional version of it. Write about coming home at noon and having your husband, or the cable guy for that matter (it's only a fantasy) pour you a martini and make wild, animalistic love to you. Who says you can't write that in your journal?

Your journal doesn't care if you're a terrible speller or that you don't own a thesaurus. It doesn't care if you have a nasty habit of letting participles dangle. Your journal is there to support and never judge.

If you need more of a reason to journal, take note of this: doctors have discovered that people who journal are healthier. They're healthier physically and psychologically. They do a better job of paying attention to their feelings and the signals their bodies are sending them.

According to a recent study published in the *Journal of the American Medical Association*, asthma patients who began to journal soon experienced better lung function, and people with rheumatoid arthritis saw their symptoms improve by 28 percent! Problems with romance? There's no research to show how journaling can tackle those issues, but just imagine the possibilities!

Worried that someone will read your private, most personal feelings? Get a lock or just put it in a place, like your nightstand, where one should be able to expect a little privacy.

The great thing about a woman journaling, though, is that even if the *initial* purpose is to write about experiences in a relationship, the juicy stuff is usually *still* buried under mounds of information about feelings, hopes, dreams—things that would likely bore any sneaky journal-intruder to tears before he ever *found* the "good" stuff.

If you're still terrified that someone else would find it and read it, do a journal on your computer (requiring your personal password) or do it online. Oprah Winfrey's website offers a free online journal because she believes so much in the power of journaling, tracking one's feelings through the written word. Go to her website at www.oprah.com to sign up. The website will keep your journal safe and *secret*. It's really a sensational public service.

So what else should you write about in your journal? Definitely write about successes and failures in trying new things with your mate. Write down your experiences. Write your feelings, hopes, dreams, and things you rarely talk about but feel intensely. The great thing about writing is that you can go on *endlessly* and your journal never gets bored or wants to talk about itself for a change.

Write about times in your life when the romance was flaming hot. Omit the names of the guilty if you choose; you'll know who you're reading about when you go back over it. Write about what's changed in your life. What's worse? What's grown better?

There's only one rule to journaling: look back at your writing and be aware of what you're expressing. If it's constantly negative, and you feel that it's not serving you well, then change your direction. You can create all the romance and magic in your life that you want, and your journal is there to help you all along the way.

4.
Romance Defined

"Love is the whole and more than all."
—E.E. Cummings

*I*f he knows me, shouldn't he already *know* what I consider romantic?"

I've heard the question more than once from my friend Ellie, who has been trying to get her new husband to be more "romantic." But after several conversations and pleas for more "romance," Fred still had no clue what she was talking about, what it was that Ellie was saying she was missing, and what it was she wanted him to do about it.

The word *romance* conjures a million different images to a million different people. Its origin might have something to do with the confusion.

It comes from the Latin word *romancius.* It means Roman, as in *words* written in the Roman languages of French or Latin. The word *romancius* was used when talking about long tales of love and adventure written in those languages. So even then it was considered something fictional, not based in reality.

These days, *romance* can be used to mean hundreds of things. Someone can say "pure romance" and it's understood that they mean "delusional." It can also mean *sentimental, sexual, melodramatic, passionate, dreamy, fantasy, idealized, preposterous, unrealistic, fabrication, sensitive, extravagant,* or *fairy tale.*

When you say "romance," nobody knows what you really mean. So is it any wonder men get that *what-language-are-you-speaking?* look on their faces when we ask, "Why can't you be more romantic?"

It doesn't help that somehow, over time, the word has taken very different paths of meaning, depending on the gender of the person you're talking to.

I emailed a male writer-friend of mine not long ago to ask him for his thoughts on romance and how couples could bring back the magic. I was stunned to receive a return email from my good friend describing scores of sexual positions and borderline kinky scenarios.

"But what about *ROMANCE*?" I emailed back.

There was a long pause. Then I could practically hear his laughter permeating the World Wide Web. He wrote, "Now I understand why you're writing this book. Men see romance *as sex*. You've got your work cut out for you!"

Well, I don't think it represents an unsolvable problem. For us to get more romance in our lives, it's not really necessary that we call an emergency session of the United Nations and forge some universal, intragender, intergalactic, uniform definition of *romance*. It's really only important that *my* husband knows what *I* mean by it, and *I* know what *he* means by it—so we stand a better chance of making each other happy.

But getting personally clear on what you mean is no small task, either. Most of us begin this process with only a hazy vision of roses and walks on the beach. Surely there are other things. There had better be, or the florists of the world are going to die of overwork and the continental shelves are going to wear down!

So sit down with your journal and think. What is it, really, that you want romantically? Include the things you can do for yourself *and* the kinds of things you'd like your partner to provide. What does romance mean to you? More dinners for two? More hand-holding? More foreplay? More baths together? More trips to exotic places? Write it all down.

Write about the little things, the big things, and everything in between. Just about anything you can think of that would bring you happiness can be considered romantic. What makes you happy? What *used* to make you happy before life got so complicated? Journaling on this will work wonders.

Once you get clarity on what romance is to you, it's so much easier to sit down with your mate and enlist his help.

You'll find that once you're clear about what you want, men are eager to do whatever it takes to enhance your happiness with more romance. Here's how the conversation went with my husband:

"Honey, I've been thinking a lot about romance lately. We've been so busy, and I didn't miss it at first, but I realize that I do now. I'm going to make a real effort to do more romantic things for myself, and for you, too, and I could really use your help. I really think I could become more passionate—like I once was—if we did more romantic things like visit the place where we first met. I'd like to spend more time at twilight with you, outside, holding hands and watching the stars come out.

"I'd like to go to outdoor cafés and drink wine and eat French bread with you. I'll plan some romantic outings, but it would mean so much to me if you would plan a few as well. If you could surprise me with flowers once in a while, it would make my week! I don't need romance *all* the time. I just need for it to be *alive* in our life together.

"I recognize that my idea of romance probably looks nothing like your idea, and that's OK. Maybe we can just respect each other's definition and help bring it about for each other.

"I promise that I'll be appreciative and not critical. I promise that once you see how appreciative I am when you do something romantic—like the kinds of things I mentioned—you'll just want to have more and more romantic moments."

Sounds like a one-sided conversation, I know. Gary really did just listen, mostly. But it worked like a charm. Not only was he receptive, he ran to get a pen so he could start writing my romance specifics down. I realized then that he wanted nothing more than to make me happy. It had always been his deepest wish. What a great romantic discovery.

5.

Honestly Romantic

*"Without outward declarations,
who can conclude an inward love?"*
—John Donne

There are some stubborn men who can adore you, practically worship you, but still not understand why they must participate in your quest for a little more romance.

"Why do I have to buy you things and do stupid things for you to show you that I love you? You should just *know* that I love you!"

Sound familiar? These are the words that my friend June kept hearing every time she tried to explain to her husband Dan that she occasionally wanted him to make a little extra effort in the romance department.

"Once in a while I wish he'd stop by at the bakery and buy me a slice of chocolate cake if he knows that I've had a bad day! Is that so much to ask?"

June deserves a lot of credit for persistence. She tried to explain to Dan what she wants about ten times without attempting to strangle him even once.

Here's a simplified approach to answering a man's questions about *why*.

I told June to try this:

"Dan, there's the long answer to your question and a short one. Which would you prefer?"

As men *always* opt for the short answer—the answer is this:

Why do you have to *buy* me things, and *do* stupid little things for me? Honestly? Because it's what I want, and it will get you what *you* want, too.

I will be so appreciative, you won't believe it. You have no idea how grateful I will be for even the tiniest act of romance. A piece of chocolate cake. A sweet-smelling vanilla candle from the check stand. A deep, slow, passionate kiss the minute you walk into the door. *Any little sign of affection will do.* All those 'stupid' little things you could do for me make me feel so cherished and will make me crave closeness to you.

Before you resist any more, please just try it. I'm going to do lots of small, out-of-the-ordinary things for you and for us, and it would just be great if you'd try it too. You wouldn't believe the mileage you'll get out of one 'stupid' piece of chocolate cake!

If this sounds too much like groveling to you, then revise it. But it's important that he get the message that there's really something big in it for him, and it's not that you're currently holding your affections hostage until he gives in. It's that you could be that much *more* passionate and loving and grateful for his existence with one little *piece of cake!*

My friend June *did* manage to get a more romantic husband. Dan eventually came to understand that little things went a long, long way with June, and he started doing them.

Be honest about what you need and get it. There's no honor in being the martyr who one day, without warning, just walks out on a relationship with a great man and perfectly good romance potential.

Now June and Dan are having their cake and eating it, too.

6.

Find Your Romance Style

"Is it not by love alone that we succeed in
penetrating to the very essence of a being?"
—Igor Stravinsky

It takes time and effort to bring more romance into your life and your relationship, but it shouldn't feel like work, another thing on your "to do" list, another reason to surround yourself with Post-it notes or the dreaded "action items" in your planner. If *that's* what it took to make my marriage more romantic, this wouldn't be a book on romance at all. It would be called *The Joy of Chastity and Solitude,* by Sister Camae Louise St. Marguerite.

Creating and building romance in your life should be fun.

It all comes down to personal romance style and personal taste. It comes down, literally, to *whatever turns you on.* Start identifying what does it for you and what's just another chore.

If you love the idea of writing love notes and leaving them around the house for your mate, wonderful. Perhaps you'd rather leave thong underwear around the house in various places for your mate. If those suggestions don't appeal to you, don't do it.

It's the journey, not the destination, that's important, so you've got to enjoy the ride however you can. I tend to think of it in the same way that I think about exercise. If you're not enjoying it, ultimately you'll quit. You *can't* quit when it comes to romance, so you've got to find a way to express yourself romantically and sexually that you really enjoy.

For some people, romance is the never-ending challenge of doing something romantically daring: wearing nothing but a trench coat and a smile to a fancy restaurant, surrounded by people you don't know. If it turns you on and doesn't harm anyone else, fabulous!

Of course, to another person, an adventure like that is neither romantic nor exciting. Perhaps to them, romance is filling the whole living room full with of flowers and candles—and not to please *him,* but rather to get *you* feeling more romantic.

If it feels like hard work, it's not your romantic style. Start discovering what *is* your romantic style by going back to your journal and jotting down a few things that you *know* make you more passionate. Not just things your partner can do for you, but things you can do for your partner and yourself that make romance feel fun and invigorating.

Romance should refill your spiritual gas tank. If it drains your energy and does *not* reinvigorate you, you just haven't yet discovered what makes you feel good and more romantic. You still need to discover your own romantic style.

What I mean by that is, let's say you're planning a romantic afternoon. You want to fill your living room with flowers and candles and a mattress on the floor and soft music—all leading up to a very wonderful, romantic couple of hours with your mate. The whole process should be fun—from cutting flowers from your garden to gathering the candles to arranging the room to finding the right music. It should *all* be a romantic buildup. When your mate comes home and you have a wonderful afternoon together, that should be the icing on the cake. The whole experience should lift you up and make you feel happy.

Romance does take effort, but the right effort will give you wings and a path to follow and express part of your true nature along the way, a part of you that's just begging to come out and breathe new life into you.

Romance—personified through you—is pure magic!

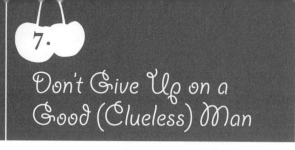

7.
Don't Give Up on a Good (Clueless) Man

"A man's womenfolk, whatever their outward show of respect for his merit and authority, always regard him secretly as an ass, and with something akin to pity."
—H.L. Mencken

ven men who are complete clods at romance can be taught and trained. Let me tell you about my good friends Ted and Tracey. They were planning for their wedding and saving every penny. Tracey knew she had a romance-idiot on her hands, but he had so many other wonderful qualities, she couldn't let him get away. But the moment of truth for Tracey came on the night of a special performance at the opera house.

With all their scrimping and saving, the romance had really gotten away from them. That's a bad thing when you haven't even gotten married yet. Tracey explained to Ted that she needed a night of real romance and asked him to take her to the opera—not just any performance, but the sexy *Carmen*.

Before the big opera night, Tracey spent most of the day preparing, doing her nails, her toenails, a facial, you name it. She dressed in red satin and looked stunning.

The night was all set. Ted was expected home at five. He'd change clothes, then off they'd go to a fabulous night of romance. At about five fifteen, Ted called and asked if it would be OK if he had a beer with one of his coworkers. He innocently (read: stupidly) suggested that she just *meet him* at the opera. With tears in her eyes, she told him to forget it, that she'd go to the opera alone. And she did. Not only that, she called off the wedding. She was convinced that Ted would never have a clue about her romantic needs, and days passed before the wedding was back on.

Now, there's something you must know about Ted. He adores Tracey. I mean, he's absolutely nuts about her. He's a hardworking guy, and any fool could see how utterly crazy Ted is for Tracey. But how could he be so clueless? And how could he not be aware that with the stress and strain of planning a wedding, it would be much easier for Tracey to snap at that time?

Tracey eventually realized that Ted's tiny flaws were greatly outnumbered by his other outstanding qualities, and she decided to give the relationship another chance and promised to be more patient with him and teach him how to be a little more romantic. She explained to him that he really hurt her, and it was a wake-up call to him. He was eager to learn how to be the kind of romantic man she wanted and needed.

Ted still doesn't resemble any kind of Casanova, but he makes a real effort and Tracey is doing a better job of explaining calmly what she needs from him.

I went to their wedding and learned he'd planned a three-week surprise honeymoon all by himself. All Tracey knew was that she was going somewhere warm and sunny. What she didn't know was that Ted had arranged, down to the last detail, a trip that would take them to every one of the Hawaiian islands, each new plane or boat trip to a new island, a whole new adventure! Tracey was so excited that Ted was surprising her. And he was clearly proud to be her knight in shining armor.

As another wedding present to her, he presented blueprints for the second-story addition he was going to build on their home. You may have to read the chapter "Utilitarian Romance" to appreciate this one, but Tracey saw it as a very romantic sign that Ted was thinking very seriously about their *building* a life together.

Through heart-to-heart talks, Ted came such a long way in such a short time. Ted has always wanted to be the man of Tracey's dreams, but without Tracey's help and patience, he wouldn't be able to find his way there.

The kind of romance we're talking about getting a man to understand is the stuff of *women's* dreams, not men's. The kind of men who make the perfect mates may not come complete with an understanding about women's fantasies and how to make them come true. They simply come with a desire to make us happy. That's a pretty great quality, and it's why we should never give up on a good, but clueless, man.

8.

Focus on Having Fun!

Ever watch young lovers? When they're not pawing on each other in public, they're doing things that could only be described as *fun*. They're the couples you see at amusement parks and putt-putt golf. It's very rare to see them at Home Depot, arguing over brass versus chrome faucet fixtures.

Relationships change over the years, and it's not long before dreamy afternoons of walking hand in hand evolve into afternoons of arguing over who is going to stay home with the kids while the other person performs the glamorous task of buying cases of Huggies and SpaghettiOs.

There's always another thing on the to-do list. The funny thing is, there were *always* chores on the to-do list. But back then, you didn't care. Stacks of laundry to do? They could wait. Bills to pay? Do them early tomorrow morning before work. The important thing back then was that you steal a few hours with your sweetheart. Those days don't have to be gone forever.

Focus on having fun again. Relax and lose the agenda. Take some time to remember what made your first dates so much fun. Sit down and have a conversation about it, focusing on what works in your relationship. Reminisce. Do you and your partner have the same weird sense of humor that no one else understands? Was that one of the things you noticed right away when you started dating? Focus on that. Go see a comedy—stage, screen, whatever. Afterward, just hang out together, basking in the afterglow of a fun night. Hold hands. Kiss in public.

Remember what you *used* to do for fun back in your more carefree days of young couplehood. Go to a wine tasting. Go bicycling and take a picnic basket. Go to an outdoor concert. Walk around the farmer's market. The important thing is that you both have fun.

Dates focusing on fun should probably include something more than just dinner out. Unless that's the activity that you most miss from your early years of dating, dinner out can be pretty blah. For some people, a date at the amusement park may be just the thing. I know it's childish, but that's exactly the idea. When was the last time you allowed yourself to have some childish fun with your spouse? When was the last time you laughed so hard with him you could feel your sides ache? Do you even remember what could possibly make you that happy?

For Shawn and Jesse, it's all about travel. They fell in love traveling through Europe together, and there's just nothing they have more fun doing than immersing themselves in another culture.

While hopping on a plane isn't something they can do every weekend, they discovered there were plenty of ways they could enjoy what they used to enjoy together by exploring new cultures and foreign lands—all within an hour of home. And so can you.

Go to Chinatown. Take a foreign-language class together. Take a class on Greek dancing together. Go to a Lithuanian cultural festival. Do the German chicken dance together at Oktoberfest. Get crazy!

Another way to have fun is to play "tourist" in your hometown and take the time to see all the things only tourists ever experience. My husband, Gary, and I have had a lot of fun ever since we decided to systematically target all the sights of our hometown of Seattle. There's so much to enjoy here. Ferry boat rides. Orca watching. Fish markets where they fling enormous salmon all around. The original Starbucks.

Making a commitment to fun may not come as easily as it once did. Sometimes it's necessary to invoke a few rules about compromise and finding something to do that you'd both really have fun at.

In my book, having fun is *not* hiking all day. That's a real bummer for my husband. Having fun for *him* is not antique hunting or garage sale-ing. Bummer for me. So when my husband and I go out on a fun date, those activities are out.

Another rule that you may have to agree to is not putting too much pressure on the "fun" date. It doesn't have to be the most fun you've ever had in your whole life. It doesn't have to be Disneyland-when-you're-six-years-old fun. It also shouldn't have to be French-café-outdoor-table-with-moonlight-and-accordion-player romantic. Just fun.

9.

Sex Over Laundry

"One must not be mean with affections; what is spent of the funds is renewed in the spending itself."
—Sigmund Freud

Laundry may not be something you think of as a giant priority in your life. But it's something we all have to do, and when you add up all the time you spend every week pre-washing stained items or sorting colors (omit both these steps from your time calculations if you're a man), you may figure that you spend at least three hours a week doing laundry—maybe more!

Now mentally calculate how that laundry-time commitment compares to the time spent on your sex life. If the laundry is winning by a mile in terms of your time and attention, that should serve as a wake-up call that you need to change that part of your romance reality.

"Sexpert" broadcaster and columnist Rebecca Rosenblat, a.k.a. "Dr. Date," insists that women should be at least as attentive to their sex lives as they are to their dirty clothes.

"You may not be in the mood for doing your laundry, but you wouldn't let it pile up for two weeks," says Rosenblat. "So why would you neglect an even more important aspect of your life?"

Dr. Date has obviously never been to my house. The laundry can easily pile up for two weeks. But her point stands. Sex is an integral part of a marriage and it shouldn't be neglected, even if we don't feel like doing it.

Rosenblat, a licensed sex therapist, points out the snowball effect that regular or irregular sex can have on a relationship. Men need sex in order to feel intimate, women need intimacy in order to want sex. Someone's got to give first and it might as well be the woman, because men will give women the world on a platter if their needs are attended to.

"If a woman is taking the initiative to be sexual," says Rosenblat, "he's going to take notice and want to reward her, stroke her, do whatever it takes to make her happy."

And after sex, a man is much more open to new suggestions about how he can make the whole experience more romantic for her next time. He'll be more open to ideas like lighting candles and bringing roses. Attending to regular sex means getting everything you want in the way of romance!

Don't think of sex as yet another chore, like laundry. But do think about it as a critical ingredient to a happy marriage, and a happy marriage being a dish that you're constantly, joyfully stirring and simmering.

10.
Control Freaks Never Get Surprises

"Surprise is the greatest gift which life can grant us."
—Boris Pasternak

*I*f there's anything better than a romantic gesture, it's one that comes as a complete surprise. But to be surprised, you have to give up some control. Very hard to do if you're a control freak. If you're undecided as to whether you qualify as a true control freak, take my simple test and check all of the following statements that apply to you.

___ *I picked out my own engagement ring.*

___ *Our honeymoon destination was gorgeous, as I knew it would be— because I picked it out.*

___ *I almost always choose the restaurant.*

___ *I don't know why some women sneer at Martha Stewart.*

___ *I think the person who invented Post-it notes should be knighted, or at least given ambassadorship to an important country.*

___ *I pick out some of my own birthday/holiday gifts. I'd hate to jeopardize a good gift-getting occasion by letting him go shopping on his own.*

___ *I named our dog/cat/goldfish/child.*

___ *I decided when it was time for cat/dog/goldfish to be put down or flushed.*

___ *My mate is considered the easygoing one. Strangely, I've never enjoyed that title.*

_____ *I often find myself secretly believing that I am one of the few intelligent people in a universe of complete idiots.*

_____ *It's not uncommon for me to write page-long instructions explaining the simplest of tasks to other people (like my mate) when they're "helping" me.*

_____ *I often feel like I'm carrying the world on my shoulders (along with three grocery bags) while wearing spike heels.*

_____ *My mate never complains about the burden of endless decisions he has to make.*

_____*One should never wash dark towels with the light towels, or you risk getting dark lint on the light towels and light lint on the dark towels. That's why I usually just do the laundry myself—far too risky to let someone else do it.*

_____ *I know (without looking) almost exactly how much money is in our bank account right now.*

_____ *I love catering, planning, and decorating for my own parties. I am a frequent hostess.*

If you said "yes" to five or more of the above questions, I think we can safely assume that you are, or should be, a card-carrying member of Control Freaks Anonymous. It's a very big club and I just know that I've been secretly elected president at some point in my marriage.

It's tough to let go of control. But for the sake of romance, it's a must. You *want* to be surprised more often. You *need* him to take the lead once in a while. Wouldn't it be nice if he planned a dinner out without consulting you, took care of the kids' arrangements, made the reservations, and just told you to put on your coat? It would be a dream come true for so many of us women who take turns carrying the world on our shoulders.

But to get a guy to take control, you have to take bold steps. You have to let him know that it would be OK, even welcomed, if he were to make a single decision about a date on his own. And most importantly, you have to be willing to appreciate his decisions and accept that it's not the *last* night out you'll ever have—so it's no crisis if things don't turn out perfectly.

The next time you're thinking about a night out on the town, ask him to make the plans and promise to be happy with whatever he chooses. He'll naturally wonder aloud who you are and how you came to possess the body of his lover. But he will probably be pleased. Be honest and tell him that you've finally come to grips with the fact that you have a control problem, and you're trying hard to let go a little. Assure him that his plans don't have to be perfect, they just have to be from his heart.

There are so many romantic and personal perks to giving up some control.

Some benefits include:

- More surprises, more often. He's going to feel empowered and more confident in his ability to make plans and make you happy.
- Relaxation. You'd be amazed how relaxing it is when you're *not* in charge all the time. Being relaxed is the first, critical step in a successful romantic evening.
- He'll get better at being romantic. His ability to make good choices about romantic evenings is going to improve with practice. But don't make that the focus of giving up control—he's never going to be as good at planning as you are!
- Freedom from upset when things don't go as planned. When you're *not* in charge, it's not *your* fault if something doesn't work out right. You have less invested.
- Improved health. Being a control freak is unquestionably unhealthy. High blood pressure and ulcers might be just the tip of the iceberg.
- Letting go of control over little things enables you to shift your focus and really appreciate the big, important things like love, family, and friendship.

When you're involved with someone who seems clueless about romance, it's tough to give up control. You may have in mind a romantic dinner with actual fabric napkins, and sadly, you end up in a sports bar, expected to enthusiastically eat a hundred buffalo wings with your fingers. That can be a real romantic disappointment. But he has to start somewhere on the pathway to romance-ville, and some just start farther away than others.

Don't forget that being a control freak has its price, too. You end up being viciously jealous anytime you hear a woman talking about how her husband surprised her with anything from flowers to a weekend away. In the end, you're only robbing yourself by trying to control too much, denying your mate the opportunities to improve and learn how to really please you.

Let him start planning some dates, some weekends away. Let him pick out and make reservations at hotels or buy takeout food without consulting you first. Allow him to resume buying horrible Christmas and birthday presents for you—in lieu of the ones *you've* been picking out (for him to give to you). Better yet, set him up for gift-buying success for life! (See: "Gold Turkey.")

Consider allowing room in your life for the surprises to come in. You'll be amazed how much you missed them and how little you miss having total control.

"Honor the ocean of love."
—George de Benneville

$\mathcal{H}$ere's an easy way to make sure you're getting, and giving, romantic attention that's really appreciated and on target for your individual needs: a fishbowl full of ideas for romantic activities.

Spend an evening jotting down little romantic things he could do for you. Have him write down the kinds of romantic things that *he* would appreciate from you. Make it a fun evening together. Have a glass of wine, listen to music—whatever you'd both enjoy as you scribble your romantic ideas onto paper. Color code your ideas so you'll know whose is whose (pink for yours, blue for his).

Try to pick ideas that can be accomplished relatively simply and with little or no planning, such as *buy me a bouquet of flowers* or *take me to a romantic viewpoint and kiss me deeply.* Both those ideas can be accomplished on any date with no planning at all.

The fishbowl full of ideas can be used for no-special-occasion opportunities to do something nice for one another or on date nights. Reach in and grab one of his blue ideas while he grabs for one of your pink pieces of paper in the bowl. Don't tell each other which ones you grabbed. Surprise each other at some point in the evening by making each other's little romantic wishes come true.

Besides instantly making dates and no-special-occasion moments more romantic, a great side benefit to fishing for love is that pretty soon he's going to get a very clear understanding of exactly what you consider romantic, and vice versa.

Don't be shocked or offended if what you and he consider romantic are vastly different. A lot of men, but not all, think of romance as *sex*. So when you ask him to write down things you could do for him that are romantic, be prepared for whatever *his* definition of romance is. Don't try to change his idea of romance. He'll likely be surprised by your idea of romance, too. It could be very eye-opening, and ultimately wonderful.

Allow each other to hold different ideas about romance. The point of learning about your differing *visions* is not that you compromise and conform to *one* vision. It's only important that you "get" your mate's vision and respect it. This is an opportunity to turn clashing opinions into a win-win situation, with him making your wishes come true and your granting of his, too.

Every now and then, take the time to refill the bowl or jar with new ideas or old ones that you especially loved and would never tire of.

Fishing for Love is a great way of telling him how he can make your dreams of romance come true without having to actually say it aloud. You get your knight in shining armor and avoid conversations altogether that start with, "Why don't you ever ___ for me anymore?"

There's no blame in the fishbowl, only easily materialized dreams of romance and simply realized signs of love and happiness.

12.

Find New Role Models For Romance

Is there anything more romantic than a newlywed couple nervous and excited about starting a new life together? Is there anything more precious and wonderful than that moment in time? You look at the couple and say to yourself, "Oh, they are so cute! Thank God they have no idea at all that seven months from now they're going to be at each other's throats."

Steven and April, both survivors of bad relationships in the past, did know how tough newlywed marriage could be. They took relationship-building classes months before getting married. They loved the experience and were excited to share some of their newfound relationship wisdom gleaned from the classes. One bit of advice they got was to hang out with newlyweds for the rest of their lives. Newlyweds, it was explained by their instructor, didn't have to *work* at being affectionate. Newlyweds gazed into each other's eyes and were sensitive to each other's needs. Newlyweds were, in this instructor's theory, the perfect role models to keep for the rest of your lives together.

I have to respectfully disagree with this one lesson. True, most of us *do* need better role models for romance and strong relationships than our parents. And while newlyweds may be great to hang out with to remember what new love is like, I have to question whether newlyweds really are the perfect role models. *Of course* they don't have to work at being affectionate! *Of course* they're sensitive to each other's needs! But statistics show that after all that affection and sweetness, at least 40 percent of them are still ultimately headed for divorce court. What kind of role model is that?

The perfect role models aren't the couples who've been married for three whole months and still somehow manage to muster the sensitivity to be sweet to each other. The perfect role models, the ones you should *really* be double-dating with, are the couples who are still sweet to each other after *fifty years* of marriage. They're hard, but not impossible, to find.

You see them occasionally. An old couple, walking hand in hand on the beach. Having fun together, laughing and talking. You see them on the golf course cheering each other on. You see them at restaurants, one giving the other a rose or a kiss on the cheek. *Those* are your role models. *Those* are the ones to try to emulate. Chances are they went through tough times. Times that lacked romance, times that lacked money and *could have* lacked humor—and they still made it through together. And here they are hugging, kissing, holding hands, and laughing. If any couples had anything to teach—wouldn't *they* be the ones you'd want to learn from?

My grandparents, after more than fifty years of marriage, took walks together holding hands until my grandpa's very last day on this earth. Grandpa Gene would bring Grandma Bette breakfast in bed. She would cook him old-fashioned meals and pies that could have won blue ribbons. He made her a cup of tea *every single evening*. It was not uncommon to see them kissing and hugging.

We, as couples in love, can learn valuable lessons from other couples in love. Choose your role models wisely and learn what you can from them. We don't even have to ask about some of the best lessons because they're there for the whole world to see.

No matter how long you've been together, hold hands whenever you can. Kiss and hug often. Laugh deeply and frequently together. Show kindness toward one another. Respect each other. Treat each other like a priceless treasure. That is what my best romance role models, my own grandparents, taught me.

Role models are important to our lives and relationships. Choose role models who speak to your own values in life. Choose role models who look happy together and who look like they've got a few years under their marital belts. Then do something bold: invite them to dinner and ask them for their secrets to a happy life together. You'll be glad you did.

You Can't Hurry Love

*"A lady's imagination is very rapid;
it can jump from admiration to love,
from love to matrimony in a moment."*

—Jane Austen

This advice is directed at all the single women who are trying to push their romance toward something more permanent: Relax. No, *really.* RELAX!

I know what you're thinking. *Easy for you to say, relax. You're already married with children. Your biological clock isn't ticking like Big Ben!*

But the thing is, so many of us rush into marriage like it's a contest to see who gets there first, and then we end up wondering why we rushed through what's supposed to be one of the most fun and romantic times of our lives. I can't tell you how many wives I know who now ask, "What was my hurry? Why didn't I just relax and enjoy our courtship rather than trying to rush him to the altar? Was I really so afraid that I was going to lose him to someone else if I didn't tie him up and hold him hostage until the priest arrived?"

There is a biological drive toward securing a mate for life, that much is certain. But I don't think it accounts for *all* of our rushing and worrying. And if you're still single, there's still time for you to salvage your sanity, regain your composure, and look at your situation with a new, more balanced perspective.

And here's why you *should* get that new perspective while you're still single: once you're married, you begin a whole new adventure in romance.

And it's a great adventure with endless possibilities, to be sure. But if you rush through the romance of the courtship, you may regret it for the rest of your life and wish you had taken the time to savor it. How many chances do you get to fall in love with your Prince Charming for the first time?

If I could start my relationship with Gary all over again, I'd spend more time just enjoying the romance of new love. I remember thinking, "He's the one! I can't let him get away!" But now I see how ridiculous my fears were. If a man walks away from you, how can he possibly be the one?

Most of my friends were all in the same race. While on the first date, we were plotting for the second. On the third date, we were deciding if their last name goes with our first name, or if we'd just keep our maiden names. On the fifth date, we were debating: Live with him first or wait it out and hope for an early proposal?

One of the common female courting rituals that's guaranteed to make you miss all romance of new love is the "auditioning for wife" routine. You've seen your friends do it. Maybe you've done it yourself. This is the ritual where the woman hides her true self, opinions, dreams, and desires from her new love as she acts in bizarre, totally unnatural ways to show the prospective husband what a great wife she'd make. *He's* not even talking marriage yet. It may be the last thing on his mind. But *she* is trying to read his mind about his fantasy wife and then live up to that ridiculous fantasy in an effort to get him to start thinking about marriage. It's embarrassing to watch, and among my own acquaintances it has seemed particularly common among girlfriends who move in with their boyfriends.

In this setting, you can almost hear the haunting voice of the soap opera announcer.

Now playing the role of wife is Lucy. Will Lucy be able to convince Henry that she is not only a great lover, but is also the ideal roommate? Will she fool him into thinking that she has no intention of cramping his style, or changing his horrid bachelor decor? Or will she ultimately crack under the enormous pressure she's placing on herself, day in and day out, with this ridiculous charade? When will Lucy finally start questioning whether HE lives up to HER standards as a lifelong mate?

The pipe organ starts playing music of doom as Lucy begins another scene filled with deception.

Women who do the "auditioning for wife" thing are especially prone to the regrets of missed romance later. One day they wake up and, while maybe not *un*happy, finally realize they skipped what should have been one of the most memorable and romantic times of their life. The mating dance.

Spare yourself regrets later in life. Now, while you're single, enjoy the romance that *this stage* has to offer. Let the mysteries and unknown outcomes dance between you. As anxious as you may be for an outcome, realize that you don't want to skip through one of the most perfectly romantic times of your life!

Don't just try to impress him, make him impress you! And while you're at it, tell him *now* how important it is that romance be a part of your relationship for the rest of your lives. Tell him what romance means to you and how you like to express it and have it expressed toward you. Teach him that romance isn't just for courtship, it's for life.

14.

Lower Your Expectations

"A man in the house is worth two in the street."
—Mae West

 friend of mine told me about a really funny email on men and romance that's been circulating. It goes something like this:

Some old-wife advice on how to have a happy, blissful marriage:

1) Find a man who knows how to tell you he loves you in a thousand different ways. Make sure he's sensitive and kind and feels comfortable revealing the love that's in his heart.

2) Find a man who can provide for you so that you will never have to struggle, never have to worry about money.

3) Find a man whose body you can worship and who first thinks of pleasing you sexually.

4) Find a man who knows how to help around the house, who doesn't just rely on you to do the laundry. Women need a true partnership in the home.

5) Find a man who is good with children, is patient and loving, and who takes the time to do the little things for them, like coach their soccer team—things that mean so much to a child.

6) Make sure none of these men find out about each other.

It's so true. Most women hold the fantasy that a man can be all these different ideals and more. The fantasy is probably fueled by the fact that many of *us* really are a dozen different women in a single day: bread-winner, homemaker, mother, sex goddess, psychologist, and taxi driver. But even *we* don't play all the roles equally well. Why is it that we expect or even want men to be able to be all these things? Having met a lot of famous people through my job in the media, I can tell you that even the celebrities who appear to be it all, do it all, and have it all are all lying. The cut-throat businessman who makes a killing in the capitalist marketplace and provides a luxury lifestyle for his family is not also the man who is absolutely faithful to his wife and sensitive in every way, romantic, loving way—oh, and coaches the kids' soccer team too.

So what's the answer? Cut him some slack, and while you're at it, cut yourself some, too. If you've got a guy with one or two great qualities, con-sider yourself very lucky. If he's not as romantic as you'd like, but he's an otherwise nice guy, some ideas in this book will help you express your romantic self while bringing him along for the ride.

Can you turn him into Casanova? Maybe. But remember why you fell in love with him in the first place. Remember to *do something romantic for yourself every day.* Then work little by little at explaining to him a few spe-cific things he could do for you to be your Romeo. Good men are willing to learn, but they'll never be perfect and we wouldn't want them to be.

Create Unconditional Romance

> *"Only passions, great passions, can elevate the soul to great things."*
> —Denis Diderot

If you want more romance in your life, make sure you're not setting unrealistic conditions. We often place conditions on our partner's behavior and conditions on ourselves—little rules we set up somewhere along the way that tell us when the time is ripe for romance. Oftentimes, these rules are destructive and make it almost impossible for the timing to ever be right.

How many women do you know who can't even think of doing anything pleasurable for themselves if the house isn't clean? I know women who've been trying to organize their closets for twelve years. Imagine if they put things like romance and pleasure on hold all that time. If you want to invite more romance into your life, you have to get rid of the rules and live for today.

We also place romantic conditions on our mates that are unhealthy, rules on when their behavior is acceptable enough to reward them with romance. If he doesn't do *this* or stop doing *that,* then he can forget about my being loving and romantic. When we start subconsciously building this list of rules in our heads, we set up romance for the ultimate failure.

Take Tom and Jenny. Tom had no clue he'd set up so many conditions for being loving. Tom is very big on thank yous. He expects to be thanked for any job he does around the house, from tiny to huge. Without those thank yous, Tom would barely speak to Jenny, let alone be romantic.

Jenny was irritated by Tom's obsession with being thanked. After all, lots of domestic duties she took on went unnoticed. She thought Tom was just being moody. She set up her own little rule: when Tom is being moody, I refuse to be loving toward him.

Instead of turning toward each other so that romance could still thrive, they both turned away. It went on this way, with resentment building, until they finally talked about what they'd done. They had made conditions for romance that set them up for failure.

Think about the rules you may have created for romance. If he forgets to kiss me good-bye, no romance? If he gets angry with me over something that's stupid, no romance for days? If he becomes obsessed with work (ignoring me), no romance at all?

People will always disappoint you. Nobody will ever live up to your spoken or unspoken expectations for long before they fail. And they'll do it over and over and over again, just as you will disappoint them. But not being perfect is no reason for romance to be banished. In tough times, invite it in and see what a difference it can make.

Sit down with your partner to talk about conditions on romance and rules that you may have unwittingly established. Make a pact to stop letting imperfection stand in the way of love.

It may seem perfectly logical not to feel loving when some of your needs aren't met. But think about the cumulative effect. How many hours or days go by without romance because of a minor disappointment? How many days or weeks would it add up to in a year? At the end of the year, is your relationship better or worse off for having silently stood your ground?

Talk to your partner about setting up better rules that lead your relationship to romantic success. Rules like "We must remember we're human and make mistakes." Or, "I will always give you the benefit of the doubt that you'd never intentionally hurt me if you'll give me the same kind of trust."

Make a commitment to unconditional romance.

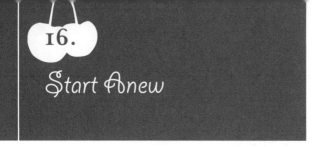

> *"Forgiveness is the answer to the child's dream of a miracle by which what is broken is made whole again, what is soiled is again made clean."*
> —Dag Hammarskjöld

$\mathscr{I}$f you've done a lot of nice, romantic things for your mate and feel like you've gotten little in return, your relationship is probably suffering from what I call romance deficit. Romance deficit is when you become angry about the inequity and find yourself withholding warmth and affection until he evens the score. Only he'll *never* be able to even the score.

I hear about romance deficit all the time from girlfriends.

"I'll make his favorite dinner, light candles, and get champagne when I know he made a successful presentation that was so important to his career. I have the lights turned low and the bubbly chilled. I make a huge effort that night to be the perfect picture of the supportive, loving wife. Do you think I get the same kind of treatment when *I* get the promotion I've been waiting three years for? Hell no!" spouts off a good friend of mine whose marriage sounds like it's headed toward thin ice. Her husband is a really nice guy who's unfortunately just this side of chowderhead when it comes to offering romantic or considerate gestures. I hope my friend learns to appreciate the good qualities in her husband and cut him a lot of slack on his weaknesses.

Men are so different from women when somebody does something nice for them. They give a warm "thank you" and they mean it. And *that's all* that's going through their heads. Unlike women, their wheels don't start spinning furiously, pondering the question *what nice thing can I now do to reciprocate this kindness?* Their brains just don't work that way (and after you read the chapter "Give for the Sake of Giving", you may start wondering whether they've had it right all along).

Keeping score on kindness and romantic gestures doesn't work. It doesn't make him more romantic, and it only serves in making you angry. We'll work on giving for the sake of giving later, but for now just consider wiping the romance slate clean. Erase his debt. Don't just do it for him, do it for you, too.

Wipe the slate clean so that the next time he does something even vaguely kind or considerate or romantic, you can feel true appreciation. You won't feel contempt or hear that evil little scorekeeper in your head saying, "Well, that's one for him. Only 266 more gestures needed to even the score."

Think about how resentment and built-up anger makes you feel. Isn't it exhausting when you think about it? It's draining to stay angry at someone. It's futile. It's self-defeating and it robs you of so much time and energy that you could be using to create a little romance in your life on your own, with books, candles, decorating, clothing, crafts, moonlit walks, or things you could do for him just because being loving is really its own reward.

If you're a romantic person, you're probably always going to run circles around him in the romantic gestures department. There's no point in keeping score or keeping track of his romance debt. Giving him the cold shoulder doesn't work. He'll just think your period is now lasting twenty-eight days a month and you'll make yourself exhausted with anger.

Wipe the slate clean and decide to be romantic, with or without him. You don't need him to create a romantic setting. You don't need him to create a little romance in your life. It's something you can do for him when you feel like it, no strings attached. And it's something you can do for yourself to honor a very real and important side of you. Start getting ideas about how you can release your mate from the bondage of romance debt and start celebrating your romantic nature every single day!

17.
Romance Every Day

*I*t takes practically no effort at all to convince a man that you deserve a little romance, a little magic, that tiny spark on a day-to-day basis. Men are easy. The real debate, the real knock-down-drag-out, scream 'til you're blue in the face, mental/verbal boxing match comes with yourself. Convincing *yourself* that you deserve *specialness* because you are indeed *special.*

The solution, *my* solution, to a lack of self-love, is to romance the self. Do one thing every single day that's special for you, and tell yourself you're doing it because you love you. It has to be really special. You can't buy yourself the same double latte you buy yourself every day and call it your one special thing.

Take the time to dab perfume behind your knees and inside the elbows and tell yourself you're doing it because you're lovable and wonderful. Make yourself fresh-squeezed orange juice and tell yourself you're doing it because you are *that* special to you. Light candles for dinner, even if you are eating alone and dinner consists of an unrecognizable frozen tray with only four grams of fat. Light the candles *especially* if you're forcing your body to digest that kind of sludge. Take a longer-than-usual shower and tell yourself that you're rewarding yourself for working so hard and for just being your special self.

One little act of romancing the self can go a very, very long way over time. Three weeks into the project, who knows? You may actually start *believing* that you're important to you and special and lovable and wonderful.

Sarah is a friend of mine whom I've always thought of as having a good self-image. But we can all fall victim to the epidemic of self-loathing. Working in the media, I'm keenly aware of all the advertising messages that seem to say *You're not good enough. You could be so much better!* But Sarah has always seemed immune to the self-hatred the rest of our friends are constantly battling, so something she said one day surprised me.

Sarah says whenever she starts getting down about herself (which is usually at the gym), she looks around at all the other people working out and says to herself, "I look OK. I'm doing pretty well. There are a lot of people here who are struggling with their weight and getting nowhere. I definitely look better than them. I guess I shouldn't feel bad about myself."

I want to shake her and say, "Sarah, it's not just that you're in shape and are looking good. That's less than 1 percent of what makes you so special! You're smart, and everyone knows it. You have a wonderful, devilish sense of humor and a laugh that makes people want to be with you. You have friends who adore you and would do anything for you. Why do you need to compare yourself to people at the gym to confirm that you're special? YOU ARE SPECIAL!"

And as I contemplate how I would scream the obvious to my good friend, I also wonder what I could say to myself. I've fallen in with self-loathing like every other woman alive today. I'm only too well aware that my body screams "I'm someone's mom!" My face is chubby, and I have the unique displeasure of getting to recognize that fact every day as I appear on television, reading the news.

How can I lecture a friend on loving her whole, wonderful self when at times it's been such an impossible struggle for me? Well, I know this to be true. Self-love begins with a single step, a promise renewed every day with a single act of romancing the self. A tiny act accompanied by the words, spoken or just felt, *I love myself.*

If you can give yourself the kind of romance and love you're seeking, it'll be a lot easier for your mate to chime in and add to the romance in your life. If you're treating yourself right, it will be so much easier for your mate to do something romantic and have it appreciated.

When we're *not* doing something romantic for ourselves every day, when we're starving for romance, a bouquet of flowers from your lover has so much to live up to. They can't just be flowers, they have to symbolize passion and devotion and longing and whatever else we're starving for. That's a lot of pressure to put on one little bouquet or one unsuspecting partner! When we *are* doing something romantic for ourselves every day, flowers can just be flowers. They're a nice, romantic surprise and that's all.

If you already believe you are lovable, it won't be such a miserable task for another person trying to convince you that you are wonderful. If there's a void, a hole in your heart where love of self should be, no one else will ever be able to fill it but you.

Take the first step in loving yourself today. Try romancing yourself. Give yourself one tiny gift of romance. It's more important that *you* romance yourself than it is for anyone else to. Do something tiny that says *I love you, I really, really do*. Then get up and do something else just like it tomorrow. And the next day. And the next. And the next.

section two

pure
romance

18.

Candlelight, Bubble Bath, and a Permanent Marker

*"Life has taught us that love does not consist
of gazing at each other but in looking outward
together in the same direction."*
—Antoine de Saint-Exupèry

Even romantic relationships need clear goals. But scheduling regular goal-setting meetings sounds as romantic as a trip to the dentist.

That's why I think more goals should be set in the tub. Get out the bubble bath, light a few candles (several, so you can see what you're writing), grab a clipboard, some paper, and a permanent marker. Climb in the tub, both of you, and start writing down goals and dreams for the future. At the very least, this should be an annual event. Maybe it could become a New Year's Eve tradition!

A very romantic friend of mine recommends you add a few non-permanent markers to the activity and write goals all over each other's bodies. How's that for making a routine chore like goal setting fun?

Why does a romantic relationship need clear goals? Many marriage counselors agree one of the reasons why there's such a letdown after a couple gets married is that with the wedding challenge over and done with, the couple no longer has an exciting goal to work toward together. We need common goals—something that's bigger than the both of us and worth working toward as a team.

One couple I know tackled the problem of post-wedding letdown long before their wedding. My friend and his bride decided they wanted to be the type of couple that other people admire, respect, and seek out for help in times of trouble. They started working toward that goal before they got married and kept on going once the "I dos" were behind them. Today, they're still on track and *are* the kind of couple you aspire to be like and *would* come to for advice about how to make it last.

Goal setting can also be a way of taking something very practical, like getting out of debt or saving to buy a house—and making it fun instead of a drag.

If goal setting isn't fun, you're not doing it right. It's dreaming with a real target in mind—a destination that will tell you when you've accomplished what you set out to do together. If talking about getting out of debt, for example, *is* a little difficult to make fun—enter bubbles. It's my experience that it's next to impossible to have a conversation go wrong amid a bath of bubbles that tower three feet high.

Set ambitious but reachable goals together, and make it mounds of fun!

Do-or-Die Date Nights

*"Never close your lips to those to whom you have
opened your heart."*
—Charles Dickens

I asked a very happy couple I know for the secret to a long-lasting and obviously blissful marriage. Date night was their answer. Every Thursday night without fail, they go on a date to the movies, to dinner, for drinks—anything, just out.

"With three kids, it's really the only time in the week when we can talk to each other and get a complete sentence out. I think it's the one thing that has kept us happy together all these years," says Mariel, one half of the happy couple.

I've heard of many couples who begin the weekly date night ritual, but pretty soon demands all around bring about its demise and date night becomes just a memory. Not for Mariel and Joe. I have to think it's no coincidence that while they're exceptionally diligent about date night, they're also exceptionally happy.

Date night is as much a priority for Joe as it is for Mariel. In fact, she tells me it's one of the reasons she married Joe. Early in their courtship, Joe told her that someday, when he was married and had kids, he was going to make sure to steal his wife away on a very regular basis for couple time.

Joe followed through with his promise, and Mariel says it's one of the keys to their romantic success. Reconnecting for a few hours every week solidifies the foundation of their family and kindles the heart-fire. They both dress up a little, making that extra effort like they did when they were first dating, and go out on the town.

Mariel confesses that their dates are not always the most original. They have their favorite restaurants and are regulars at the movie theater.

"Sometimes it is a little routine, but I have to say it's never boring. I wouldn't give up date night for anything in the world. It's the only time we really get to enjoy one another's company. It's kept us close."

Date night is very romantic. It inspires all the romantic feelings that Mariel says she needs to feel on a regular basis. Because her needs for romance are satisfied, Mariel says she's much more interested in romance on a sexual level, which keeps her husband much happier, too. Taking time to reconnect makes all good things in a relationship possible.

So take it from Mariel and Joe, date night is not some cliché ritual. It's a necessity, a key ingredient in the recipe for long-term romance.

20.
Get Him Dancing

*"Marriage is not a ritual or an end. It is a long,
intricate, intimate dance together and nothing
matters more than your own sense of balance
and your choice of partner."*

—Amy Bloom

*I*magine twirling around the dance floor with your own personal Fred Astaire. Would you settle for waltzing in cautious circles with a nervous and self-conscious Fred Flintstone?

Contrary to popular belief, it *is* possible to get the Fred Flintstone type to take dancing lessons with you. I read in a recent "he said/she said"–type article in a popular women's magazine that it just flat out couldn't be done. The "he said" part made it amply clear, in no uncertain terms, that real men would *never* be willing to take dancing lessons with their mates. But I'm telling you from experience, if you want something badly enough, you can *always* broker a deal.

I asked my very own Fred Flintstone–like husband (OK, he's a *little* more progressive than that) what it would take to get him, and other men, to participate in dancing classes. He said, speaking for the men of the world, that he'd be willing to join me, under very strict conditions:

1) Dancing *class*—not classes. Sign him up for *one* class, with the option of taking one more (and so on), once it's determined that said class is slightly less painful than an appendectomy without anesthesia. Also, he wants to know that he can take classes as desired, as opposed to feeling the dread of knowing that every Saturday night for the next eight miserable weeks is already all planned out for him.

2) Private lessons—not a class. He doesn't want to feel humiliated in front of a whole room full of strangers who now know him as the idiot with two left feet. He has no desire to mingle with other happy couples, especially other men who are deranged enough to be interested in participating in a dance class.

3) Input on dance type. It has to be okay for him to say "yes" to waltz, and "hell no!" to swing dancing, depending on his personal preferences. He doesn't want to have to argue about it with you in front of the instructor or worry that you and the instructor are going to gang up on him and pressure him into a dance style that he doesn't want to learn. Agree in advance the types of dance you'd both be willing to learn, and stick to it.

4) Let's make a deal. He's doing this for *you*. Now you offer to do something for him. For every dance lesson he takes with you, you agree to participate in another activity of his choice.

Those are the rules, according to my husband. Gary insists that if you religiously follow the above guidelines, you will get your dance lessons with your mate.

"If a guy has some say in the details surrounding the lessons and if there's a great enough reward in it for him, I don't know any guy who wouldn't agree to that," Gary said.

What about this *reward* business? Gary says for him to agree on dancing lessons (and he has), the payoff would have to be something like my agreeing to go hiking with him or chartering a boat for a day to go fishing on the ocean. To put it mildly, I was stunned by this request.

"You want *me* to go fishing with you? Why would taking someone who doesn't fish at all out to the ocean to go fishing for a day be fun for you? Why, of all people, would you want to go fishing with *me?*"

His answer was simple. "So you could watch me catching fish and think I'm the coolest guy in the world."

"Fine. Deal. You've got a deal. One dance lesson for one day of fishing."

Never mind that his logic makes no sense to me. I didn't bother telling him that I already think he's the coolest guy in the world, and that fishing will neither hurt nor help his image. And I left alone the fact that I would *hate* a day of fishing, sitting around waiting for some innocent fish to get caught and bonked on the head on the deck of the boat until they're lifeless and pathetic. We have to make sacrifices for the things we want most in life, and I want dancing lessons.

I don't care if we never look like Fred and Ginger. I'd settle for looking just slightly more sophisticated than a couple of bumbling, pubescent junior high-schoolers. If that means convincing my husband that watching him catch a fish will really elevate his image in my mind—so be it.

Let the dancing (and fishing, I guess) begin!

"A man who does not love praise is not a full man."
—Henry Ward Beecher

A very romantic friend of mine confided that she's embarking on a mission to fulfill one of her husband's most raw, primal needs. It's a need that she knows can lead to more romance for her and a happier marriage all around: heavy praising.

"He wants it. He needs it. I know he needs it. But sometimes I feel like I'm dealing with another child when it's so obvious what he wants. I'm drained from taking care of our kids all day, and I don't have the energy to coddle him, too."

Susan and I talked about our husbands' constant cravings for praise and how their need is so similar to *our* need for romance. Until the men get lavish praise, they're not as interested in being the kind and romantic husbands that they could be. Until *we* get the romance we want and need, we're not very interested in fulfilling their needs for praise or sex or whatever.

I asked Susan what her husband, Mel, specifically wanted to be praised for.

"Everything. Anything he does well, any chore he accomplishes, any favor he does for me, any routine task. Just everything."

It's pretty much true for all men. They want to be praised for cleaning the garage, doing a good job on a work project, ordering take-out food, looking handsome, straightening up the living room, and simple home-repair jobs. They want to be praised for being good husbands and good fathers; they want praise for bringing home the bacon and being good all-around providers and protectors—for all these things and more, our men want lavish praise. They need it, and when they get it, they can be the men of our dreams. My husband, Gary, goes so far as to say that praise is a man's single most romantic need.

With their needs for heavy praising met, men are more romantic, more interested in fulfilling all of our romantic fantasies (provided that we're willing to praise them for that too, of course). Susan and I decided that it was worth the investment.

We made a pact: from now on, we're going to work on delivering our husbands' needs for heavy praising, and we invite you to join in our mission.

Is it ridiculous that we have to praise our men for tiny little chores done well when half the things we do around the house and out in the world get unnoticed or fulfilled by the "domestic fairy"? Yes, absolutely absurd. But then, our needs for praise are not as great. *His* needs for romance are not as great, but he'll fulfill them anyway, happily, if he's getting all the things that he needs.

You know it's true. You've seen it work for you before. But maybe, like Susan and me, you've been stubborn about it, unwilling to heap on the praise, perhaps worried that it won't sound sincere. It doesn't matter if it's sincere. He won't notice and won't care.

Think about it: when we get a dozen roses, do we ask ourselves, "Did he really mean to send me a dozen roses?" Of course not. We're just happy to get them and couldn't care less about his sincerity. Likewise with praise. He needs it and doesn't care if you really mean it from the bottom of your heart.

Invest in heavy praising and watch the dividends come back to you in romance. Fill his deepest needs and watch him work hard to do the same for you.

22.

Breathe In Some Moonlight

What is it about moonlight that puts us in the mood for romance? Is it because it's always new, always changing? Is it because of the perfect light it casts when it's full and round? Whatever it is, it's a fascination that men and women share, making it a perfect place to start when you're trying to add more romance to your relationship. Take the time to simply gaze at the moon together!

You can also choose to take moon gazing to another level together. Look on your calendar and take note of when the new moon comes. Ask your lover for a date on the new moon or full moon. If your calendar doesn't have any lunar information on it, buy a new calendar that does. Or just look on the Internet.

What I love about having a date with the moon is that we don't need a baby-sitter, just our porch swing and a clear, cloudless night. Sit outside with your partner and just gaze. Let the conversation flow or let the moment be wonderfully silent. Hold hands. Kiss. Think or talk about your dreams for the future and what you're grateful for right here, right now. Pray together. Lean on each other. Take some deep breaths. Sigh.

Looking at the moon is a form of meditation. It clears your mind and rejuvenates your spirit. A lot of people meditate by the clock. They say, *For the next thirty minutes, I'm going to let myself just be.* Set a watch alarm if you'd like. The reason I suggest the alarm is that some people have a tough time doing nothing. If I didn't set a little alarm, my husband—even though he *likes* moon gazing—would probably give it about five minutes then go back inside to check the score on the baseball game. This would definitely ruin the moment for me. If we decide in advance that we're going to gaze for thirty minutes, we will both surrender to the moment.

It needs to be said, however, that you don't *need* a lover to have a romantic moment in the moonlight. It's nice, but not necessary. Just ask any wife of a man on military leave, away for months at a time. Sometimes you have to create your own romance. A little moonlight can do that. A cup of chamomile tea can make the moment even better.

Add your own extras when it comes to moon gazing. Sometimes a little music is right. But sometimes it's nice just listening to the sound of the hemisphere settling in for the night. Relax and romance. It's hard to get moon gazing wrong.

For information on new and full moons, the Internet is a sensational resource. The U.S. Naval Observatory can tell you what the moon will look like on any given day up to the year 2035! Just go to their website (www.usno.navy.mil) and type in "phases of the moon" in a quick search (it's a huge website). Using their lunar calendar is a great way to plan for many romantic nights of moonlight.

Happy gazing!

23

Designate a Special Place

"God gives all men all earth to love,
But, since man's heart is small,
Ordains for each one spot shall prove
Beloved over all."
—Rudyard Kipling

My parents-in-law, very happily married for more than thirty-five years, have always had a special place to celebrate their relationship. They have a cabin in the mountains of Wyoming a mere twenty minutes away from their home.

Over the years, they've used the cabin as a way to get away from it all and to be with each other. It's also a place where they've marked special moments and celebrated birthdays, anniversaries, and major holidays. All the beloved dogs they've ever owned are buried around the cabin. They've been snowbound there, gone there for consolation, and commemorated major milestones, too. It's *their* special place.

Not all of us are lucky enough to have a cabin in the wilderness to call our own, but we can designate a special place. It could just be a camping spot or a cabin regularly reserved. It could be one special hotel room where you go to celebrate big moments.

It doesn't even have to be an overnight destination. It could be a special table at a favorite restaurant, or a park bench in a beautiful spot with a view of the whole world. It could be one stretch of beach where you go to walk and talk about important things together. It could be a sailboat or ski-boat where you go to enjoy life, togetherness, and the open waters.

When I think of my in-laws and their cabin, I think of the comfort of permanence and tradition. Continuity. Over the years, they've moved from one house to the next, watched their sons grow up and acquire homes and families of their own. The one thing that has stayed the same is their special place: their cabin.

Every couple could use a special place to which they can return and hold sacred for their whole lives together. A place where you can at once get away from it all and revisit the most important moments of your life together. A place for romance and sentimentality. A special place, just for the two of you.

24.
Go On a Romantic Hayride

"Flat country seems to give the sky such a chance."
—Dodie Smith

I love the idea of a romantic hayride, gazing at the stars on a quiet rural road far away from the chaos of the city. Many times I've seen this idea for a date in magazines or websites and chuckled, thinking (as I sit in my house in the suburbs of Seattle), *Where the heck am I going to find a hayride these days?*

Answer: they're almost impossible to find, except around Halloween in some places. However, many old, family-run farms are making a comeback as tourist attractions starting to offer fun, old-fashioned activities like hayrides. You may have luck finding farms like this in your region. Finding a twilight hayride is a little more difficult.

But a romantic hayride isn't impossible to create on your own. In fact, it's really easy if you can borrow or rent the right vehicles. You'll need a car with a trailer hitch and a flat-bed trailer to pull behind. Utility trailers are fairly easy to find and borrow/rent out in the country. Just buy someone a beer and be friendly and they'll loan or rent you their trailer.

Straw can be bought by the bale. Stack the straw at varying heights in the utility trailer. Hire someone to drive the truck at five miles per hour through the rural area and there you go!

If it sounds like an awful lot of trouble to go through for one date, make it a triple date. Make it a theme party. Tell your friends you're all going on an old-fashioned hayride and combine resources. Each couple can take their turn at driving the truck.

Too embarrassed to make out in front of all your friends? This is why it's best to get the biggest utility trailer you can find. The bigger the trailer, the more you're able to stack those hay bundles at varying heights in an irregular pattern. Pockets of privacy abound.

Be sure to play some slow country music in the truck. The experience just isn't the same with Madonna or Bach playing.

Hayrides are best on clear, cloudless nights so you can watch for shooting stars. Be sure to bring blankets and wear long pants. Straw is scratchy—but very, very romantic.

Write Your Own Fairy Tale

"When you love someone, all your saved-up wishes start coming out."
—Elizabeth Bowen

When you first fall in love, you think it would be impossible to forget those critical moments when you first *knew* this was the start of something real, something wonderful. Every moment you fall deeper and deeper seems so intoxicating, yet so vivid: how could you forget a single second, let alone the thousands of reasons for falling so hard?

But as you settle into a relationship and resume the day-to-day chores that take up so much time in your life, the memories get pushed back, as Barbra Streisand sings, to the corners of your mind. It's even possible that you one day forget completely why it is that you fell in love at all. It's especially easy to forget during harder times or during an argument.

To keep the romance alive, you sometimes have to dig way back into your memory bank and remember why it is that you first fell in love with each other.

I guarantee there were some very special reasons you were attracted and you both fell in love. Can you remember what they were?

Take your mind back to your first meeting and remember what you first thought about him. Maybe the attraction wasn't instant. But there was a moment when it first clicked. Can you remember what caused the click? Was it something he said? Something he did? The way he smiled?

When it all starts coming back to you, write it down—every detail you can think of. Write it in your journal and let the memories flow back in.

Once you've put your memories to paper, you may wish to do something more with the story. You can just copy edit your love story, or you can rewrite it completely as a fairy tale. Take the memories you've written down and rework them into the type of story, poem, or detailed journal entry that you wouldn't mind reading over and over again.

The purpose isn't necessarily to create some family heirloom that your children can read to their children about their grandparents' love story, although that's certainly a possibility.

The purpose is to create a written account of any kind that will trigger old feelings and, during difficult times or wonderful times, help you remember *why* you fell so hard, so deeply in love with your mate. There were special, magical reasons.

Writing down your love story will help you when you're angry, when you can think only of negative qualities of your mate. Let's say your mate is terribly unorganized, and it's been progressively driving you nuts for months and you're starting to feel like you really want to throw him and his scattered papers and laundry out on the street. Revisiting your love story will remind you that the reason you fell in love with him was because he is so creative and expressive. He, while completely unorganized, is the most sensitive man you've ever met—giving with his emotions and love and creative with his expressions of passion.

You are awash with memories as you read your love story, memories that remind you that before he stumbled into your life, you were trapped in a little, boring, organized world. Then suddenly, this burst of masculine creativity and sensitivity, a rare combination indeed, burst in, leaving you changed, and fascinated, and totally in love...forever.

How would *your* fairy tale read?

I'll share with you one memory from my own love story—the moment when I absolutely *knew* this was the man with whom I'd spend the rest of my life.

It was our first official date, though I'd been falling for Gary for months. His charm, his good looks, his laid-back style—how could I *not* fall for this man?

But the moment I "knew" wasn't that unusual of a moment. We were walking through a very crowded party. It was a retirement party for a local firefighter. So crowded was the room, I was sure every fire code was being violated.

Suddenly the rest of the room blurred before my eyes, as I watched him move through the crowd. There were old ladies and gentlemen to his left and right, and I watched how gentle and patient he was...aware of his great size and strength. He gently braced people as he walked through. It took him forever to make it over to me because he was so careful of the people around him.

I don't know if his obvious gentleness was so special to me because I'm petite and have been knocked over so many times by bigger people. Maybe it was just his kindness that suddenly became obvious to me.

Whatever it was, that was it. That was the moment. I knew that I could live the rest of my life and never meet a man such as this ever again. He was the one.

And, years later, as I reread these words, I realize Gary is still the same gentle giant I fell in love with.

Sometimes I get frustrated, being a Type-A personality, that Gary seems to be moving too slowly for me, literally and figuratively. But then, I reread the fairy tale of our love and I realize that he's the same gentle soul that had me mesmerized at that party. He is patient and gentle and good. It's why I vowed to love him forever that night. It's why I still love him today. It's why I will love him thirty years from now and forever after that.

If I were to forget that night, I might forget the very things about Gary and our love story that are most important.

Write down your love story in whatever way feels right to you. Do with the story whatever is enjoyable and meaningful to you.

To some people, the memories may be so personal and private, the story may travel no farther than a locked journal.

Others might find it fun to print their fairy tale, then mat and frame it for others in their home to read. Some might turn their story into a little bound book that gets passed down to children and grandchildren.

Do what feels right, but whatever you do—*remember*, and spend time with your memories.

Memories have magical powers and can keep the magic of love alive.

"The city has a face, the country a soul."
—Jacques de Lacretelle

I've always thought bike rides are romantic. Not the Lance Armstrong–type rides at breakneck speeds, but the slow, lingering type that allow you to relax and even talk to each other while you're riding.

Find a country road in flat farmland and go for a bike-riding date. I say *flat* only because if it were very hilly, I would end up bike riding alone with my husband about four miles ahead.

Look for the dreamiest country road you can find. Whenever I'm searching for a new bicycle route, I always think of the Country Time Lemonade commercials. They always show kids riding through the prettiest country spot you've ever seen. I don't really care much for lemonade, but I love that commercial and want to find that spot!

Be sure to pack a picnic or figure out where a little café is on your route. Pack lots of water, and then just hit the road.

Don't go for speed; take in the scenery and sounds. Let all the competition cyclists pass you by.

Wave to everyone. It's expected in the country. People on tractors and in cars will be ready to wave back. Don't ever snub the country people; these are the folks who'll be driving you to the hospital should you tear a hamstring.

The ideal country cycling route would have a river or lake nearby so you can stop for a swim if it's hot. It at least should have a patch of grass where you can lie down and gaze up at the clouds and trees.

Let go of your agendas, your "to do" lists, all your troubles. This bike-riding date is all about being together, lowering your blood pressure, taking in some fresh air, and cleansing yourself of all the things that cause you stress.

I think of the cycling trips as a seasonal romantic ritual. We only go about twice a year when there's the most daylight available.

Cycling dates ground us and remind us of what's really important. The ground, the sky, the land, each other. The trip reminds me of simpler times, just like the lemonade commercial. Simpler times when summer was relaxed and carefree and being together was all that was important.

Marooned At Home

"Stay, stay at home, my heart, and rest;
Home–keeping hearts are happiest."
—Henry Wadsworth Longfellow

Send the kids off to Grandma's, turn the phones, faxes, and pagers off, and put a *Do Not Disturb* sign on your front door for a weekend. Don't check your email. Consider yourself marooned.

We've all become so easily accessible to the outside world, but so inaccessible to ourselves and our lovers. It's time to reconnect during one very private weekend. No shopping. No golfing. No appointments. Just the two of you "snowbound" in the house or backyard. A full forty-eight hours, privately dedicated to your couplehood.

You can make love, watch old movies, read the newspaper, read a book you've been meaning to get to. You can spend a little time just nurturing each other.

If anyone asks you what you're doing that weekend, tell them you're just not available. Tell Grandma and anyone else who deserves to know that you're having private, undisturbed couple time. I wouldn't tell too many people this, though. It's none of their business.

Being marooned means being able to make love on the couch at one in the afternoon. It means being able to take a two-hour bubble bath without interruptions or guilt.

The toughest part about this weekend will be scheduling it together. Finding a free weekend (when you can get baby-sitting, if you have kids) isn't easy. *Keeping it* is even more difficult. At least ten things will come up that will beg you to reschedule. Don't.

Think of it as emergency periodontal surgery—it can't be rescheduled. In fact, if you like, *tell* people you're having emergency periodontal surgery. Both of you. What are the odds? What horrible luck! And yet, you'll be well enough to care for yourselves, but sleeping a lot, so please observe the sign on the door. If you're not sleeping (you tell them) you'll take down the *Do Not Disturb* sign and turn the phones back on. But there will be blood (throw in diarrhea, just for good measure)—the kind of unpleasantness you wouldn't want to subject anyone else to. And you've already stocked up on yogurt and Pepto-Bismol, so there's really no need for assistance from others.

It's best not to tell this white lie to anyone who is a resolute "helper," especially those with a spare key. But at least that'll solve the problem of why the office will not be able, for once, to reach you 24/7.

Imagine all the romantic possibilities of a whole weekend marooned at home! Isn't it worth all the lies and deceit you can muster?

28.

Give for the Sake of Giving

"Love is, above all, the gift of oneself."
—Jean Anouilh

any women love to give. It makes them feel good to give, whether the giving involves a gift or just time. It's sad that giving has become a battle of the sexes and a major issue in the war for equality. If you love giving, what does it matter if the receiver isn't very good at reciprocating? Was getting something back the point of the giving? Of course not. If giving makes you feel more happy and loving, do it.

Here's where this advice is coming from: once upon a time, I was a bride who delighted in surprising her new husband with little gifts from the heart. I'd see a sweater, note that it was his perfect color, and buy it for him. He was in my thoughts all the time, and somehow those thoughts materialized into little gifts I'd find just about everywhere I went. Months later, I realized that I never got gifts or anything, really, in return. It started eating at me. *Wasn't I on his mind? How does somebody get thirty-five gifts without it dawning on him to give a little something in return?*

It was maddening and one day I just stopped buying things for him. But it didn't make me happier. In fact, I was miserable. I never realized how important this expression of love was to me. While Gary showed his love in other ways—car maintenance, lawn-mowing, gutter-cleaning—I had robbed myself of a major way I enjoyed expressing love: giving. I started giving again, with one major change: I recognized that giving was also a gift I gave myself. I no longer needed him to give me some obligatory gift in return.

In recommending a return to giving, please understand that I'm not endorsing selflessness in any way. There is good giving and bad giving. Good giving is when it makes you feel great and leaves you with enough for yourself. Bad giving is being a martyr—sacrificing more than you're willing to sacrifice without a shrine being erected in your honor. If you're sad or disappointed when the moment of giving is gone, that's a sign of giving gone wrong.

When you embrace good giving, you let go of the "score." For romantic women, keeping score robs you of a lot of joy in living. If you make him a wonderful meal with all the romantic trimmings of candlelight and champagne, make that moment your own reward. Don't expect the reward to come later with a reciprocated act of romance: a box of chocolates or a romantic night that *he* plans. Most people will disappoint you if you're waiting for them to reciprocate in just the right way.

Women are naturally better at giving and reciprocating. It's what we're taught from birth. Boys just don't get the same education in giving, and it's not their fault. Over the years, a man may learn how to be a great giver, but the score may never be even. So let go of it. Let go of the need for an even score and just give until it feels right to you, and stop when it's bothering you.

As my close girlfriends and I get older and wiser, we too are letting go of the need to reciprocate with each other. We've made a pact not to buy each other Christmas and birthday gifts. We have made it OK to buy each other the rare gift that stands out, but only with the promise that it must not be reciprocated just for the sake of reciprocating.

It sounded very practical when we made the pact. We all had too much stuff already. Obligatory gifts just added to the stresses of the holidays. We didn't want to do that to each other.

But I think the reason we made the pact goes deeper than the practical reasons for it. We care about each other and don't need gifts to prove it.

I wonder why it is that many of us are more reluctant to release our lovers from meaningless gift obligations in the same way. Is it because we've always felt the score pretty even among our close friends and miles apart with our lovers? Are we, somewhere in the depths of our hearts, really angry that it seems like they don't even *try* to give as much as they get? If that's the case, is the solution to silently pressure them into giving in a way that's as unnatural to them as it is natural to us?

Wipe the slate clean on giving, then make a new pact with yourself. You will give if and when it brings you joy. You will give without a thought about getting. You will give without care for gratitude beyond a simple "thank you."

Promise that you'll take care of yourself first, and then give of what is left. Being a giver doesn't mean being a martyr. When you take care of yourself first, you end up with more to give others.

Women understand the spirituality of giving. We know that giving, from the moment of its conception all the way to its completion, is an act of love that brings us closer to God. Keeping score is a violation of the sanctity of the giving. It keeps true love, true joy, at a distance.

Really romantic giving comes from a place in your heart that is perfect; a place that knows *love* is the only true reward.

"Thou art to me a delicious torment."
—Ralph Waldo Emerson

He loves it when you sneak up behind him and put your arms around his waist. You go crazy when he kisses you unexpectedly on the back of the neck. You learned these things while dating and they were ways you could create romance and a loving moment in an instant. What a great thing, that special thing you do.

But time goes on and life gets more complicated. It seems like coordinating a time to have dinner together requires two secretaries and federal mediation. Maybe it seems like it's been months since the last time you walked up behind him and hugged him, or the last time you were surprised with a back-of-the-neck kiss. What happened? It takes maybe five seconds and doesn't obligate either of you to a full-blown romantic interlude. Yet we, for some reason, stop doing those things we do.

It could be that we stop doing those things without even thinking about it. Maybe we stop because we notice that it's been a while since he's done *that thing* for us. Whatever the reason, it's a pity that we would let something slip away that's such an easy way to reconnect.

Well, bring it back. Start hugging him from behind, or nibbling on his earlobe, or running your fingers through his hair, or whatever it is that defines *that thing you do*; start doing it again—today. Do your part and it won't be long before he's back to kissing your neck, rubbing your shoulders, kissing the inside of your wrist, or whatever it is that he does that drives you crazy. If he has forgotten, simply remind him. If you've resumed doing that thing you do, he'll be happy to oblige.

Find new and creative ways to create instant romantic feelings. If you come home and discover he's in the shower, climb in fully clothed, and spontaneously do that thing you do. He'll think you're crazy and wonderful.

Isn't it amazing how something so simple can mean so much? It means so much to him that you remember what he loves, what makes him feel loved, and it sparks a physiological/romantic response every time. When he kisses you in that place, or holds you just right, doesn't it make you feel like you're not just being sparked sexually, but being sparked by your soul mate? He's the person who knows you and loves you better than anyone else in the whole world. That's what *that thing you do* means when you do it, and he returns the favor.

Bring these physiological and psychological triggers back. Find something that reminds you of that special thing, and place it somewhere in your common living space. Something as simple as a refrigerator magnet. You could buy a refrigerator magnet that's as simple as a little pink heart, put it on the refrigerator and program yourself to remember that the magnet symbolizes that special thing you do for your mate. Something like that can be used to remind you not to forget to do that thing you do often and with love.

You don't want to do it so often (more than once a day) that it loses its magic. You want it to stay magical and never to get taken for granted. Once a week might be perfect. Find your own special formula for doing that thing you do in a way that drives both of you crazy and keeps you in the mood for love!

30.

Live Vicariously Through Josephine

*"Home late tonight. Meeting. Don't wait up.
I'll grab a hamburger. — Love, X"*

I f the above comes close to the *most* romantic letter you've received lately, you're probably feeling a little romance starved, and rightly so. Rather than getting angry or frustrated, why not just steal a little time for yourself and create a little romance on your own?

One of the best and easiest ways to bring romance into your life is to start reading more and activate the part of your brain that relishes romance.

Find a literary romance genre that works for you. Some like a touch of mystery. Others are strictly Jane Austen. Some prefer memoirs. And don't forget another source of great romance: letters.

Some of the best romances in history have left us wonderful letters to remember them by. Among the best are the letters from Napoleon to Josephine.

Reading his letters to her, you can feel his intense, almost crazy love for her. OK, he was just crazy in general, but that doesn't make his letters any less romantic.

Consider what he wrote in April of 1796, when he was begging Josephine to come see him just days after they were married. He was near Italy commanding the French army, and he begged her to come to Milan.

I have your letters from the 16th and 21st. There are many days when you don't write. What do you do, then? No, my darling, I am not jealous, but sometimes worried. Come soon; I warn you, if you delay, you will find me ill. Fatigue and absence are too much.

Your letters are the joy of my days, and my days of happiness are not many...But you are coming, aren't you? You are going to be here beside me, in my arms, on my breast, on my mouth? Take wing and come, come!

A kiss on your heart, and one much lower down, much lower!
B.

So she was married to a power-hungry, obsessive freak. So what? The upside to all that obsessiveness is that she got some darn good letters from him that exist even today and provide a glimpse into one of the most notorious and passionate romances in history.

If you too would like to live vicariously through Josephine, there are a number of books that contain the translated letters between the famous couple. Among them are two books by Sandra Gulland, published by Scribner's. *The Many Lives & Secret Sorrows of Josephine B.* and its sequel, *Tales of Passion, Tales of Woe* chronicle Josephine's experiences before, during, and after being the obsession of the military master of France.

Another great collection of letters come from pre-revolutionary Russia between the last Tsar and his wife. Tsar Nicholas and Tsaritsa Alexandra had a fairy-tale-turned-tragic love story that lives on through the hundreds and hundreds of letters they wrote to each other through some of the most important and turbulent times in history.

Their letters are much more tender and loving than the mad passion of Napoleon. They also provide an intriguing glimpse at World War I behind the scenes. The two wrote to each other almost every single day, detailing all the important political and military events. But my favorite parts of their letters reveal their pet names for each other and how they worried about and loved each other so dearly and genuinely.

Sept. 19, 1914

Lovey dear, my telegrams can't be very warm, as they go through so many military hands—but you will read all my love between the lines.

...I commend you into our Lord's safe keeping—may He guard, guide and lead you and bring you safe and sound back again.

I bless you and love YOU, as a man has rarely been loved before—and kiss every dearly beloved place and press you to my own heart.

Forever your very own old Wify

June 3, 1916

My beloved angel! How I long for you, thirst to see you, to kiss you and to talk to you! I feel that I shall soon ask you to come here for a few days to enliven us all with your charming presence. God keep you and the girls! I press you tenderly to my breast and cover you with countless kisses, my dear old Wify.

Yours Eternally,
Nicky

It's amazing that all the letters survived the Russian revolution and were preserved for the ages. After the revolution, journalists published bits and pieces to a public that couldn't get enough. But now, with the Internet, it's so easy to be able to indulge in this romance for yourself. One of the best websites I found was The Alexander Palace Time Machine at www.alexanderpalace.org/palace/, where I got the above excerpts. Not only can you read hundreds of letters on that site, you can see pictures and learn about the love story involving one of the most fascinating families in all of history.

Sadly, you may never get your lover to write such impassioned letters. But you probably also won't be held captive in Siberia or die of a broken heart while your lover is in exile on the island of Elba.

Find some romantic letters and indulge in the fantasy of being the worshiped muse of a king or emperor!

31

Play "Love At First Sight"

*"To be loved at first sight, a man should have
at the same time something to respect and
something to pity in his face."*
—Stendhal (Marie Henri Beyle)

Agree on a common meeting place, like an upscale bar, and pretend you don't know each other; let him make the first move and let the sparks fly just like it was the first time.

Before you start thinking this is just the typical one-night-stand-with-a-stranger fantasy in disguise, hold up. *This* acted-out fantasy is much, much better. Of course, the stranger fantasy is great, in a raunchy sort of way. But the *love-at-first-sight* fantasy is fun in a much more romantic way!

What's the difference? The stranger fantasy usually involves a couple of drinks, a suave guy with unquestionable intentions, and like ten minutes worth of dirty talk before you leave—hoping to shock a few onlookers by the notion that two strangers could actually hook up and head for a bed after only one-and-a-half margaritas. News flash: no one's shocked. People with loose morals are everywhere, it's the people with virtue and class who are really shocking to see.

The love-at-first-sight fantasy is so much better. It doesn't require the thrill of having spectators, though it's the type of thing that really does attract attention. If you've ever seen two people falling for each other in a public place, you know that it's impossible to take your eyes off them. And everyone wants to believe that love at first sight really does exist.

So here's how it works. It starts out the same as the "stranger" scenario. Only after a few drinks you catch each other's eyes (I know, still sounds very similar to the "stranger" thing, the differences are subtle at first) and he moves in, slowly. *Slowly,* because he cares. He doesn't want to screw it up. You respond politely, nicely, but not aggressively, for the same reason. Try to remember what it was like to see someone for the first time and really think, *Hold everything! This one could be really special!*

When you first meet someone really special, you don't think about jumping them; you want to get to know everything about them. They want to get to know everything about you. You stare into each other's eyes, you try to say witty, intelligent things.

People who think they're instantly falling in love aren't trying to pick up on a person; they're studying them. If you've ever seen it happen, or ever experienced anything like love at first sight, you know that it's like staring at someone so intently as if to engrave their image onto your mind forever.

People who are falling in love don't ask each other sexual questions; they say things like, "Please don't tell me you're married." They say, "So where could I find someone like you on a typical Saturday afternoon? What do you like to do with your free time?" They ask, "Can I take you to dinner—anytime, anywhere?"

The great thing about *this* love-at-first-sight encounter is that you know you won't get your heart broken. You can be bolder and more open with your heart than you would *ever* allow yourself to be in a real first meeting.

How do you get your man to play along? Have him read this chapter. Tell him it's only three pages long.

And guys? You know that it's almost every woman's fantasy to be swept away by a knight in shining armor—here's your chance! You have *no idea* how much it would mean to a woman to have this fantasy really played out. Women dream of not just *any* man, but the *right man*—YOU— sweeping her off her feet. Be brave enough to be a fool for love.

And here's another tip: as you're acting out the love-at-first-sight fantasy, remember to stay in character *all the way through.* Try to pretend it's the very first time. And not the first time with *just anyone,* but the first time with the woman with whom you're convinced you want to spend the rest of your life. A woman you *cherish*. That means putting her on a pedestal, worshipping her a little bit. She will do the same for you and will follow your lead. She will treat you like a god that she wants to worship forever.

Make this fantasy come true for her, and I promise, you'll be repaid tenfold. Anything you desire is yours.

There's nothing like the first time. And there's nothing like seeing a stranger and knowing, just knowing, that he or she is the one.

32.
Champagne Romance On a Domestic-Beer Budget

There are thousands of ways to cut corners on expense and still have a wonderfully romantic date.

Most people don't take advantage of many free events in their home towns. Every year, giant corporations get pressured into sponsoring countless free concerts-in-the park or theatre-under-the stars. Every year, cities spend thousands of dollars to create free events that make their cities more appealing, but very few people hear about the events.

The trick to finding them is simply reading the weekly Arts and Entertainment supplement (usually out on Thursdays or Fridays) in your local newspaper. Don't just read the articles, read the advertisements. Events are usually advertised. They're also usually on a city's web page or the parks and recreation web page. You just have to train your eye to look for those kinds of notices.

It's not just cities and counties, but companies as well, that throw free parties and events they want you to attend. If you're a wine lover, read everything on the web pages for the local wineries. Ask to be on their mailing list.

There are dozens of free opportunities every week in your area to listen to top-notch music, watch wonderful entertainers, or taste some of the best foods your area has to offer and take part in some old-fashioned community hoe-downs. Don't assume that the best entertainment and the best kinds of dates require big bucks; some of the most romantic fun in your area can be had for free!

33

Go to the Drive-In

"The car has become a secular sanctuary for the individual, his shrine to the self, his mobile Walden Pond."
—Edward McDonagh

obody has to tell you why drive-in movies can be so romantic. They're sweet and nostalgic, reminding you of a time when life was a little simpler and cars were a little steamier.

But you probably didn't know that there are hundreds of drive-in theaters still operating all around the country.

The best way to find out where there are drive-ins in your area is to check out the website www.driveintheater.com. Run by drive-in enthusiasts and theater owners, this website will not only tell you state by state where the operating drive-ins are, it will also tell you about all the ones in your area that have gone under over the years and interesting facts about when drive-ins reached their peak in popularity state by state.

There are only a few states that no longer have any drive-ins. I was actually shocked to learn that there are thirteen theaters still operating in my home state of Washington. They don't advertise, that's for sure. You really need a website like the one mentioned if you're ever going to find the few remaining drive-ins and take advantage of this old-fashioned, romantic date.

One reason I've really grown to love the idea of a romantic drive-in date is that it's so easy to take sleeping children with you. You don't have to worry about getting a sitter. You've got the kids in their pajamas ready to fall asleep in the back seat, and you just might be able to find a few minutes to kiss in the front seat.

But drive-ins are great for every couple, not just desperate, romance-starved parents. Drive-ins are a place where you can legally park and kiss for two hours without anyone bothering you. Or you could hold hands, or turn the volume down and talk, or (gasp!) even watch a movie together.

Check out the website, and then go to a drive-in movie theater. Help keep the few that remain in business by telling all your friends about it. If you take your kids to the theater, you'll be able to teach them about another time in American history, and you will build memories that will last a lifetime.

For you, the benefits might be a trip down memory lane and certainly some very romantic, very steamy, very hot-popcorn buttery nights of romance!

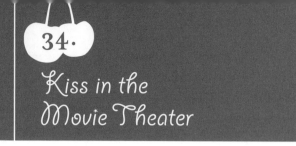

34.
Kiss in the Movie Theater

"A lover without indiscretion is no lover at all."
—Thomas Hardy

Nobody wants seats in the back row of a movie theater except very considerate tall people and couples who want to kiss. When was the last time you were one of those couples (not the tall ones, the kissing ones)?

You don't have to completely miss the film you've shelled out big bucks to see to participate in a little back-row kissing. Just kiss during the previews for the other movies and during the credits at the end.

If you're exceptionally shy or conscious about kissing in public, then just hold hands and look into each other's eyes. Take a moment to reconnect while sharing ridiculously priced candy. Kiss his hand. Kiss his ear. Do something that makes you feel, even for just a fleeting moment, like young lovers again.

Going to the movies is a great way to escape into a fantasy world. We all need an escape once in a while. It's healthy. It's important. And movies can help fill that need and give you something to do on your date nights. But rather than just going to the movies and then coming home, look for one tiny way to make your movie-land escape more memorable and romantic. If you can't kiss in the back row of the theater, how about getting to the theater a few minutes early and making out in the parking lot, arriving to see the movie thoroughly disheveled?

Unless you get a little creative about your night at the movies, there's not much of a chance for a couple to talk or reconnect, so do it in other, nonverbal ways. Make the most of it, and make it romantic!

35

Travel Destination: Unknown

"The unknown always passes for the marvelous."
—Tacitus

W hen you're thinking about taking a short, romantic trip for two, consider making it really spontaneous. Imagine going to an airport and just getting on the next flight to any-where. No reservations, no schedule, no idea what you'll do for the next few days. It's probably the only way you'd ever take the time to see some of our country's lesser-known cities just large enough to have an airport.

It's a perfect adventure-for-two with all the possibilities for great romance if you both embark with a carefree and fun-loving attitude. You may not get to stay in a five-star hotel. You may be *forced* to stay in an expensive five-star hotel. But who cares? Think of it as an adventure. I'm sure secret agents aren't able to make hotel reservations months in advance.

For couples whose idea of wildly impetuous is going out with no din-ner reservations locked in, this could represent a giant step toward fan-tastic, crazy, young lovemaking. It's all about feeling free again. Free to step outside who you *think* you have become and to become more your-self than ever before.

There's some really romantic symbolism here if you look closely enough. As couples, we set out on a journey together, not really knowing where we're going, but promising to be loving along the way, and to keep a generally good attitude about it, even when a wrong turn is made or a bad hand dealt.

The other benefits to a "destination unknown" voyage is that you aren't placing expectations on each other for good trip-planning. If the hotel doesn't turn out to be perfect, you can't blame him, he can't blame you. One fight averted right there. If the town turns out to offer nothing in the way of entertainment, so much the better. You'll be forced to entertain each other.

Hopefully you'll arrive in a town that neither of you knows much about, that way neither of you is the tutor, neither the pupil.

Ironically, it became clear me how important a trip like this could be for a couple seeking romance after planning a trip with a girlfriend of mine. We wanted to catch up and just have fun away from our families. At first we thought Las Vegas. But then I thought, you know, there are so many distractions at Las Vegas. So much to see, so much to do. What I really want to do is just talk and hang out with my friend. I don't want anything to stand in the way of great conversation. And then it hit me—why didn't I ever think about a vacation with my husband the same way? Why isn't the top priority of a vacation with him just to reconnect, too? Why do I let Grand Canyons and world-class shopping and museums that go on for miles stand between us when we should be reconnecting like best friends?

After the trip with my girlfriend, I talked with my husband about our best and worst vacations ever. Our conclusion was absolutely clear: we needed to rethink the vacations we took together. It's one thing to go to Disneyland as a family. But when we're trying to relax and reconnect, we need to look for destinations that better serve that purpose. One of our better vacations was in Maui. Lots to see and do there, but you don't feel guilty if you just sit around on the beach sipping mai tais. But there are probably lots of places we haven't discovered yet that could be just as romantic, just as relaxing.

Consider making your next trip a travel-destination-unknown trip. Take what you get and see as much, or as little, of your destination as you like. Take it easy and take time to reconnect. Make sure there's room in your agenda for the kind of romance that happens when two people are relaxed, rested, and rejuvenated. Let the spontaneity of it all propel the romance to new heights. Be like kids again and have fun together.

36.
Midnight Train to Romance

> *"My heart is warm with the friends I make,*
> *And better friends I'll not be knowing;*
> *Yet there isn't a train I wouldn't take,*
> *No matter where it's going."*
> —Edna St. Vincent Millay

If you or your husband spend half your life on a commuter train to and from work, this may not be the best idea for you, but for the rest of us, train travel can be wonderfully romantic and a trip that takes us out of the ordinary and into the exotic.

Splurge a little for a special date—you deserve it. And when you do, consider booking a sleeper car on one of North America's very romantic trains and rail lines for a special date for two.

Ever since I saw the movies *North By Northwest* and *Silver Streak,* I've thought there was something magical about time spent on a train, speeding across the plains of our great country.

I must admit, I am a snob when it comes to certain types of travel. I *do* want the upgrade. I don't consider booking seats next to herds of other people sleeping in their chairs all that romantic. I like the private sleeper cabins. I like the fancy dining rooms. I love the very quiet, first-class lounge car. Call me an elitist if you will; I don't care. I've traveled by train the other way, and believe me, there's no comparison.

A wonderful weekend rail-date could start with hopping on a train Friday evening. Go straight to your sleeper cabin, and arrive very tired from too much romance the next day in a place where the romance continues with a special dinner, some sightseeing, and then back in the sleeper cabin for the train ride home.

Here's another tip when it comes to train travel: don't be set on the time you want to get there and the time you want to return. Everything is sort of wishy-washy with train schedules. Just plan for it. Train travel is absolutely wonderful when you really don't have anywhere you *must be* in the next twenty-four-hours, if ever.

This is not the best date on which to buy expensive opera or baseball-game tickets. You don't want to spend your whole time on the train hoping that it actually gets there and looking at your watch counting the minutes the train is behind schedule. Much as I love trains, things often (read: *always*) go wrong. But if you don't really care about getting there, if the *journey* is more important than the destination, the whole experience is delightfully romantic. In fact, if you get stuck because of some problem with the tracks, it's like a free bonus! It's like having airline trouble trap you in Tahiti for a few days longer! (OK, not *that* good, but still.)

It's also absolutely critical that you not just book your travel on any old train. No two are alike, and a few in each region are designed to offer premiere train travel for travelers who know better.

For example, on the West Coast, it's the Coast Starlight train. Period. It'll take you between Seattle and Los Angeles with many stops in between. There are other trains that'll take you to the same places, but none in such style.

From New York to Florida and a zillion beautiful points in between, it's the Silver Star that you'll want to travel on.

Also on the East Coast and traveling from New York to New Orleans is the Crescent. From Montreal to New York and back is the Adirondack. From Chicago to Seattle, the Empire Builder. From Chicago to San Francisco, the California Zephyr. Also look up the Southwest Chief and the Sunset Limited.

Train travel is obviously slower than a flight, so you're not going to go for a weekend to Florida if you live in New York. But you could go to historic Virginia. You could go to Montreal. If you're in San Francisco, you could pick out a town along the rails to Chicago and stay for a romantic night. And San Francisco is an easy (read: *longish*) trip from Seattle.

One of the great guides you'll find is *USA by Rail* by John Pitt, who has traveled seventy thousand miles of rail lines in the USA and Canada. He offers great advice on more than five hundred destinations in North America and which trains you should take to get there, plus tips on buying tickets and booking reservations. Did you know that you have to make reservations well in advance if you want to eat in one of the fancier dining cars?

Given a little guidance from an experienced rail enthusiast, train travel can be wonderfully romantic, and it's certainly not something you do every day, so it's bound to set the stage for a unique romantic experience.

37

Hand-Write Letters

"More than kisses, letters mingle souls."
—John Donne

This is one way a clever friend of mine keeps the art of romance in her life alive, even when she's between boyfriends. Jean sends beautiful, handwritten letters and cards.

There's always something special about Jean's cards. Sometimes it has a pressed flower glued on it; sometimes it's more like a little decoupage design. They never look like they took hours to make. They're simple and lovely. A lot of friends compliment Jean on her cards and letters.

"I buy the best cotton paper I can find," she says, revealing what she considers her *secret* to great correspondence. It's not the fine paper (but it doesn't hurt). It's the love. How can I explain it better than to say that when I open an envelope and see a little flower glued onto the card that I know she found on a walk somewhere with her pug, Betty, I feel the love that she intends to send my way?

It also makes me think about how wise she is. In her busy day full of errands and work and doing for others, she takes ten minutes to nurture her soul by being creative and loving all at the same time.

What's amazing about it is how she creates romance in her life with paper, a flower, and ten minutes without going completely overboard, like so many of us are apt to do.

Jean's is a story of simple romance. Jean knows how to find the love in her heart and bring it out with a little paper and a purple pen. From her heart, to her hands, to the world. Pure love. Now that's romantic.

38.
Take Every Opportunity to Hold Hands

"All mankind love a lover."
—Ralph Waldo Emerson

Holding hands may never be as exciting as it was that first time in your youth when you held out a cautious paw, your heart racing, your hand clammy, afraid of rejection and utterly fascinated with this new thing called love. Handholding, when that's as close as you've been with the person physically, is wonderfully exciting.

But we get older and so does holding hands. By the time you're an old established couple, it may even seem silly to link up like that, unless there's an actual *need* for it, like when you're walking through a crowd of people and you're worried about losing each other.

Holding hands, though, is one kind of touching that's acceptable anytime, anywhere. Touching of any kind is what keeps us younger, both mentally and physically. It's another way to connect that doesn't require words, doesn't demand that everything is perfect in a relationship. It just is what it is, and it's beautiful.

I look at couples walking together, maybe visiting an outdoor market or window shopping, and I have a different feeling about the couples I see holding hands. A couple *not* holding hands may be just as much in love, just as committed to their relationship, but they look different from the couple connected by the hands. The handholding couple is moving more as a unit. One may be leading, the other following, but there's still that connection. They're definitely going somewhere together. They're telling the world that they are of one heart.

There's a gentleness, a protectiveness in holding hands. One can't stumble or even stop to look at something without the other having to be aware. There's a patience in holding hands. If you're willing to hold hands with someone, you're willing to wait for them. You're willing to take an interest in whatever interests them at the moment.

Holding hands may seem juvenile. It may seem like it's only for the young or the newly involved, but it's really forever. Holding hands goes far deeper than what you see on the surface. It has deep meaning and, I believe, deeper power in a relationship than we realize.

Take the opportunity to hold hands whenever you can. Be willing to speed up or slow down or stop altogether in order to keep that connection. What could be more important?

For many months of the year in some climates, it's not practical to have your bare hands out in the cold, dangling between your two warm bodies. I've always thought it was especially romantic to see women with their hands in their mates' coat pockets, the warmth of the fiber and his hand keeping hers warm. But there's also a fairly new product on the market that you may find even more romantic. It's called the "smitten mitten," and you can order it on several websites. It's a mitten for two, shaped kind of like a heart with an opening at either end so that a couple can hold hands in perfect warmth even in the coldest of temperatures. Buy one for yourself and give one away as an anniversary or wedding-shower gift.

We join in relationships because we have a powerful need to be with someone. We don't want to face the world by ourselves. But many people who are in relationships still feel like they're all by themselves, lonely, isolated, and cold. Holding hands can help cure that feeling of isolation.

You may not be able to make your relationship perfect. You may not be able to solve every argument or agree on resolution. You can't change each other's flaws, and you never know what tomorrow will bring. But you can hold hands and face it all together. Holding hands is a silent, effortless way of connecting and making the world a little warmer and more personal, together. It's an easy way to be loving and very romantic.

39.

Buy Bridal Magazines

Once in a while, splurge on a big, fat bridal magazine. I don't suggest this because I think you'll enjoy flipping through page after page of hideous bridesmaid dresses (do they make any other kind?). I say this because the articles and vacation packages offered are geared toward new lovers.

There's one obligatory article in each issue of these magazines devoted to "marital myths" and accepting the idea that marriage isn't *all* romance and that it requires effort and hard work to keep the relationship strong. Depending on where you are in your relationship, you can read *or* skip this article.

Other chapters invariably include romantic ideas, tips, sex talk, and honeymoon activities. Read all those.

I also love the vacation sections that take up the last third of the magazines. It's almost all advertising, and includes some of the most cheesy romantic accommodations you'll ever find. Rotating beds with heart-shaped hot tubs. Champagne-glass-shaped hot tubs with heart-shaped beds. Safari style rooms with swinging vines that plunk you into heart-shaped hot tubs. I don't know why, but the hot tub is considered *vital* to honeymoon romance.

I would never in a million years have chosen one of those tacky hotel rooms for my real honeymoon. Who needs a rotating bed when your stomach still does flip-flops every time he enters the room? But now that I've been married for several years, these really obnoxiously romantic vacations seem *perfect*. You're sure to be surrounded by young, kissing couples everywhere—not to mention all the hot tubs!

I also like bridal magazines because they remind me of the starry-eyed bride I once was. I'm glad I've grown up, but there are some dreams I never want to let go. Dreams about planning for a beautiful life together. Dreams about carving out a tiny nook of paradise for a home. Visions of our values really embodied in our life together: children, faith, family, friends.

Everyone has their own dreams, and I bet each person is reminded of a different one when flipping through the pages of a bridal magazine. It's something you may want to try, indulging in pure, innocent bridal fantasy. You might be just one *Modern Bride* away from bliss!

40.

Gold Turkey

"Presents, believe me, seduce both men and gods."
—Ovid

*I*t's imperative that you find a store or two where your man can walk in blindfolded and buy you a gift you'll like. This advice comes from a woman who suffered years of strange gifts before figuring it out.

I got a toaster oven one Christmas instead of the engagement ring I was expecting. Gary's excuse was just acceptable enough for me to resist throwing egg nog in his face. He thought it would be cheating to buy an engagement ring for a Christmas present, like he'd be shorting me a gift. It still doesn't explain why said gift ended up being a toaster oven.

One year I got some strange face-scrubber kind of device. And one time, I got a gold unicorn pendant, like you'd buy a ten-year-old girl.

And then there was the year of the "Gold Turkey." I was thrilled to be opening a jewelry box, and the jewelry inside seemed to be beautiful and unique. A square pendant with a crescent and star on it. Beautiful, but something seemed strange right away. Familiar but foreign. I finally realized that I was wearing around my neck—the flag of Turkey. We are neither Turkish nor have we ever been to Turkey, though I hear it's really a wonderfully interesting place. The star and crescent on the flag represent Islam. It's a beautiful symbol, but we're not Muslim, and to wear it felt disrespectful to its religious significance.

Enough! I had to find my poor husband an easier way to buy presents. He was killing himself trying to win at a game he's just not very good at.

Finally, I took him to a few stores where he could not go wrong. I realized he could buy me just about anything in the Ann Taylor store, or at Anthropologie, or Restoration Hardware. He simply could not go wrong there. There are also three or four local boutiques that I love. Gary didn't know about any of them.

So one day, I took him to my favorite stores, careful to avoid anything resembling a department store (men go crazy in department stores—too many decisions, too many things).

Instead of acting put out by the shopping trip, as I feared he would, Gary was absolutely fascinated. He paid very close attention to the exact location of the stores. He was mystified and thrilled that I was telling him that he could buy anything (*anything?*) in that store and I would almost definitely like it.

If crummy gifts have been a sore spot in your relationship, stop waiting for him to figure it out and help him. Take him by the hand to a store where he can't go wrong.

Ask him to take you to a store where the same thing is true for him. We like to think of ourselves as master gift givers, but we don't always get things they really *want*. A lot of times we buy things for them that we think they *should* want. There's a big difference.

Yes, it is the thought that counts when it comes to gifts. But if gifts have been standing in the way of some good holiday romance, solve the problem once and for all.

> *"There is a pleasure in the pathless woods,*
> *There is a rapture on the lonely shore."*
> —Lord Byron

Searching for a date idea that promises to be unusual, special, unforgettable, *cheap*? Plan a romantic date around the wonders of nature, and I guarantee you that it will be a date you'll remember forever.

Of all the dates I've been on with my husband, my favorite was one that didn't involve a fancy dinner or musical, but a wondrous show that nature staged for us.

He told me to dress warmly and get in the car. He wouldn't tell me where we were going. It was twilight, and I remember having no idea what to expect.

We arrived at a park in our town that I'd driven by a thousand times but never walked through. He led me to a clearing in the park surrounded by lush acres of forest.

We laid down a blanket and he instructed me to look up. I raised my eyes to the darkening blue sky. It was a clear night, not quite dark enough yet to see stars.

Suddenly I saw a dark thing swoop and flitter. Then another. Then another. In an instant, we were surrounded by hundreds of bats flying within a few feet all around us, eating their nightly feast of mosquitoes and moths.

They flew with amazing precision. It was exhilarating! It was breath-taking. These amazing creatures were expert navigators on an exact mission.

Since we were motionless, they couldn't have cared less about our presence—and displayed absolutely no aggressiveness toward us. On the contrary, I felt wonderfully protected by these winged wonders, eating all the mosquitoes that would otherwise be eating *me*.

I felt, at that moment, a wonderful connection to nature and to my husband. It was a moment I will never, ever forget. How did Gary know that I would love this? How could I thank him for leading me to something so extraordinary?

I know that a "bat-outing" isn't right for everyone. To some people, I'm sure that the words *bats* and *romance* will never be found in the same sentence. But there are a million different ways to have a romantic date that also connects you with nature. Find the recipe that's right for you. Here are some other ideas:

- Go bird watching in spring when birds are busy building their nests.
- Deer watch in the forest. Bring binoculars and stay very, very still.
- Find out about bald eagle or osprey nesting sites in your area. Watch how hard they work together to feed their young.
- Find a salmon creek and watch them jump, swim, and writhe their way against the odds and the current just to spawn in their native grounds (in fact, many communities are desperately in need of local volunteers to do regular "fish counts" in the neighborhood streams, so if you're community-minded, you can pitch in).
- Find a public garden that's popular with the butterflies. Sit together and just watch the dance of the butterfly in the breeze.
- Take an outdoor class on wild edibles indigenous to your area. I took a hike with a family once whose four- and five-year-old children could correctly identify all the edibles versus inedibles. It's information you hope you'll never need to know, but you might be thankful you do!
- Hike a well-known trail at night. Wear orange reflective gear so you'll be visible.

- Attend a "star party" organized by a local astronomy club. Clubs usually organize events around special sightings, like the appearance of a comet. Contact your local science museum for more information.
- Identify the special natural wonders that are unique to your area. In some areas, it's the mountains. In other areas, it's the Northern Lights. Some places are famous for butterflies. Swifts (birds that fly in formation) are amazing to watch in some cities. Discover what's special where you live.

Getting close to nature reminds us that we are a part of nature. Watching birds make a nest together is extremely romantic. It's impossible to do this and not feel like holding hands with the one you love.

42

Fake a Power Outage

"It is so much easier to tell intimate
things in the dark."
—William McFee

Remember how much fun it was when you were a kid and suddenly the power went out in the middle of a storm? Initial panic was followed by digging through drawers and closets for candles, matches, flashlights, and batteries. What starts out as an annoyance eventually turns into a moment that everyone savors and enjoys so much, there's disappointment when the lights flicker back on.

Power outages are wonderfully romantic, and there's no reason why you can't "fake" one and get the same feeling of roughing it in your own home.

If you have kids, there's no need to exclude them from this romantic night. It's so much fun for them, too. Turn the lights out. Light some candles, build a fire, and just enjoy each other's company. You can read together by candlelight, play games, or make shadow puppets. You can tell add-on stories or just talk about dreams for the future.

Friends of mine have actually created the same power-outage effect by renting a beach house and ignoring the instructions for how to turn on the electricity when they arrived for their trip.

Roast marshmallows, make s'mores, drink hot chocolate. Cuddle under a blanket. Play footsie. Leg wrestle! Play Twister by candlelight! Play cards, or just snuggle together.

A Native American legend says that when friends sit around a fire talking about the good things about each other, as the fire dies down and the embers glow, the friendships are renewed and sealed once again. You can use this time, while the fire dies, to renew your love. Share what you're feeling or talk about the good things that have happened lately.

We spend so much time talking about the bad things, we forget how lucky we really are.

With the power out and calm beginning to prevail in the darkness, children get sleepy faster than usual. Suggest they go to bed a little earlier and tell them they can read by flashlight if they like.

With the kids tucked away and starting to doze, the moment is ripe for romance!

43

Be Gracious About Gifts

"A gift, with a kind countenance, is a double present."
—Thomas Fuller

My Grandpa Tom has given my Grandma Alice the same brand of chocolate-covered cherries for Valentine's Day for the last sixty years. My grandmother hates chocolate-covered cherries. It's a running family joke.

Before becoming an "old" married woman myself, I wondered why she was so gracious about accepting them. Why didn't she tell him? He has to notice at some point over six decades that *he's* the only one eating the chocolates!

Being a wise woman, (far wiser than myself) my grandmother understands that it really *is* the thought that counts, especially when it comes to presents from husbands. She says she'd rather have a box of chocolate-covered cherries every year than nothing at all on Valentine's Day. She doesn't want to screw up a good thing.

I think this is a really tough romantic lesson to learn. It *sounds* good. "It's the thought that counts." But what if gifts show little or no thought at all? What if the gifts your partner buys for you appear to have been purchased for a total stranger? How do you deal with that and not get disappointed? Not get angry? Accept it with the grace and gratitude of Grandma Alice?

Perhaps it was easy for Alice to accept useless gifts with grace because there wasn't anything in the world that she needed. Growing up on a ranch in North Dakota and surviving the Depression, she's always felt extremely lucky to have anything at all. Anything beyond a roof over her head and food on the table is an unbelievable extravagance to her. Even if it's chocolate-covered cherries that she'll never eat.

Alice has taught me that all I need, I already have, and anything else is a bonus. Gifts are wonderful, even if you'll never eat them, wear them, or use them. When you thank your mate, you're not thanking him for the gift, you're thanking him for the gesture.

When you accept gifts with graciousness and appreciation, you get more gifts. Men love to do something successfully, and they'll keep on doing what works. Gratitude never goes unrewarded. That may just mean more truly crummy gifts, but it also means that he's thinking of you more often, trying harder to make you happy.

At some point, you may be able to casually draw his attention to a favorite store in which he could almost pick out a gift blindfolded and get it right. See the "Gold Turkey" chapter for more details.

Where's the romance in crummy gifts? The romance is knowing that he tried to do something kind and sweet. The key words: he tried.

If the tradition of Valentine's Day was not centered on gift-buying, but rather on something like, say, running ten miles to show a lover that you'll push yourself to the limits for them, my husband could run a marathon for me. If our materialistic culture suddenly shifted toward thinking once again that daring, athletic feats were romantic—my husband would win the prize and my heart all over again.

It's a silly example to use, but it does make me think how unfair it is to judge anyone's romantic qualities based on something in which they have no practice and that doesn't really have anything to do with romance in the first place. You shouldn't have to be a world-class shopper to be considered romantic. It's what our culture has done with every holiday and special occasion: made it a test of shopping skills, mall endurance, and wallet flexibility!

Romance *is* about the thought. Thinking of someone, showing them with some token that they are close to your heart. Accepting gifts graciously and with gratitude is a big step toward achieving the romantic relationship we all want.

44

Paddling to Paradise

"A lake is the landscape's most beautiful and expressive feature. It is earth's eye; looking into which the beholder measures the depth of his own nature."
—Henry David Thoreau

When you're trying to come up with an idea for a romantic date that will help you reconnect, don't think elaborate and expensive: think cheap. Think about the kind of creative dates you concocted when you were very young and had no money at all. One of my favorite cheap dates is a canoe ride at dusk.

If you have access to a canoe or row boat and an accessible body of water nearby, you've got all the makings for a romantic cruise for two.

Of course, rowboat and canoe rentals are usually only available during the daytime. And some lakes require that after dark you display proper lighting—so you don't get accidentally mowed over by a much bigger vessel. But on the smaller lakes, nighttime paddling is allowed and pure magic.

There's something fantastically romantic about taking a canoe out at dusk—just in time to see the last daylight and watch the shift change in the world of wildlife. From a canoe, you can see things you wouldn't normally see. Birds making their last forage for the night to feed their babies as they go to sleep. Birds and bats that are nocturnal are most visible at dusk. You can hear the owls come to life. Frogs and crickets start singing their love songs to the females of the lake and wetlands.

Take your canoe date one step farther and plan it for the evening of the summer solstice or a full or new moon. In this way, you can make the date not just a time for romance but for spiritual reconnecting, too.

Of course, you don't really have to have a boat to enjoy a natural, romantic setting at night. A blanket on a special lakeside or riverside spot can be just as nice. In order to see and hear the evening nature around you, you're forced to speak in a whisper, and that's wonderfully romantic all by itself.

Sitting and doing nothing but listening to the evening activity in nature forces you to slow down, to be in the moment, to be one with all around you. As you both slow down, sitting there quietly, maybe holding hands or hugging as you enjoy the serenity of your surroundings, you may even feel the strange sensation of your hearts starting to beat in synchronicity.

There is great romance in nature. The more you use it to reconnect, the more you start to notice and appreciate the little mating games that go on every night in the wilds of your own backyard. You start to recognize that very little actually separates us from the ducks on the lake who stay faithfully close to their mates. In nature, it's not always about romance; it's about a partnership, being a team. We can watch the birds and see that it's all about working together to build something that you couldn't accomplish alone.

The next time you're thinking about creating a date just for reconnecting and being super romantic, consider shunning the bright lights of the city. Leave your satin dress and pantyhose at home. Leave your money, too. Some of the best, most romantic dates in the world only require a blanket and bug spray.

45

Write Love Letters He'll Remember Forever

"We lay aside letters never to read them again, and at last we destroy them out of discretion, and so disappears the most beautiful, the most immediate breath of life, irrecoverably for ourselves and for others."

—Johann Wolfgang von Goethe

Goethe thought that all personal letters should be kept as a sacred remembrance of one's soul. It really makes me wonder, when was the last time I put to words *anything* that revealed my very breath of life?

A friend of mine has convinced me that more people should discover the romance of writing love letters. He has one of those marriages that everyone envies. When Jack mentions that the fifteenth anniversary of his and his wife Elisa's *first date* is coming up soon, all the women around him sigh a deep sigh. The men sit there and wonder what all the sighing is about.

So it might not initially sound so surprising that Jack also writes his wife love letters, until he explains his writing process.

"It's not easy for me. I'm not very expressive in that way. I have to write a whole lot of drafts before I feel like I've gotten it just right."

I wondered, what would make a person who struggles so much with writing and expressing make a habit of something that's bound to be such a monumental chore? Here's what Jack told me:

My dad wrote great letters to my mom. You'd never know it by meeting the guy. He didn't seem like the kind of man who'd have *anything* romantic to say. But when he was overseas in World War II, he would write these beautiful, flowing letters to my mom, whom he'd just started dating. She says she fell in love with those letters and it made her fall in love with him, too.

It taught me to not be afraid to express myself. So now I write Elisa love letters on special occasions. I'll write them when I'm away on Air Force reserve duty. I'll leave them in a special place for her or I'll mail them. I try to find nice quality paper, so that it might be something she'd like to keep.

Part of why Jack tries a little harder than most to express himself may also have to do with the fact that this is his second marriage. He learned the hard way that words of anger are expressed too frequently and easily, and words of love are too few and far between. By the time you figure out what's missing, it might be too late. So Jack made a promise to get it right this time and reveal what's in his heart. He's been able to do that through love letters.

Jack says it doesn't matter to him that Elisa isn't as into writing love letters as he is. He says she finds a hundred ways every day to show and tell him how she feels.

It's also important to note that Elisa never asked Jack to write her a love letter. It's something he did on his own. I think it's something we should all try to do on our own, not expecting anything in return. But by writing a love letter from the heart and not putting any expectations on your partner, you just might find that you inspire them to write a return letter. If not a letter, you might find them at least inspired to express themselves romantically in a way that's right for them. Either way, it's a win-win. It feels great to give a love letter, even if you get nothing in return. Love is its own reward.

The written word lives forever. And the great thing about writing down your feelings is that you can make sure you say what you want to say just right. It's a chance you don't always get when you're speaking. One misstep in a conversation and you can accidentally kill the romance. But love letters give us a chance to speak uninterrupted and say what's really in our hearts.

Give it a try. Find some special stationery and make the whole experience as romantic as you like. You can write with one of those funny pens stuck to a giant feather plume if it makes you feel more romantic while you're writing. Make it fun, and when you're finished, give the pages a spritz of your perfume. Make it something that he (or you) would like to tuck away and treasure forever. Maybe someday your children will discover them and get to feel your presence and the warmth of your love once again. A love letter is a gift that lasts forever.

section three

sexy stuff

46.

Naked Bill Night

"The undressed is vulgar—the nude is pure."
—Robert G. Ingersoll

I heard about Naked Bill Night from a friend of mine, and it's such a great idea I had to share it.

At least once a month, Sarah and Ned get naked and do their bills together. Apparently it helps them get their bills done on time every month, and three times as fast! A stack of bills that would normally take a full hour to get through, they've polished off in twenty minutes flat! And then, it's time for FUN!

I really have to admire this kind of ingenuity. They've taken a chore we all dread and turned it into something they actually look forward to. In fact, they can't wait to do their bills every month.

As they write those checks and lick the envelopes, the anticipation of being done and moving on to other things builds. By the time they're done with the household finances, they're actually chasing each other and racing to the bedroom! When was the last time you raced each other (naked) to the bedroom?

Of course, other friends tell me that Naked Bill Night would lead them to financial ruin, but what a way to go broke!

With a little discipline, this ritual could be a big boost to your romantic and financial life.

47.
Read Trashy Novels Aloud

"Some books are to be tasted, others to be swallowed, and some few to be chewed and digested."
—Francis Bacon

Read trashy novels aloud. To each other. Yes, really. And I'm not talking about porn, just your run-of-the-mill, grocery-store literary trash. The reason I say this is that if you've ever read any serious erotica, you know that they often skip the romance and move straight into hard-core sex. It's often more frightening than inspiring. But dime-store novels, on the other hand, are just good, trashy fun.

Why read trashy novels aloud to each other? Many reasons, the first being that it's impossible to talk about your household's ever-growing laundry problem or death-row furnace while reading a trashy novel aloud. It's also a great way, when your time is limited, to skip dinner and a movie and move right into intimacy. You don't even need a baby-sitter, just kids who are asleep or very occupied with anything that isn't dangerous.

But the best reason of all is that reading trashy novels aloud can bring a playful spirit of romance back into your relationship. It frees you to act out fantasies that you might never express otherwise. With a trashy novel, you can act out fantasies by just reading them aloud with feeling. You can skip the fantasy costumes and elaborate scenery, unless you're really into it. But if you're the type of person who *doesn't* feel stupid dressing up like a turn-of-the-century Bavarian milkmaid just to heat things up in the bedroom, you should be *writing* a book, not reading this one.

Reading trashy novels aloud to each other allows you to live out the fantasy, minus the costume, with a sense of humor and no humiliation. The more melodramatic, the better! As the heroine rips her dress off, to expose only her laced corset (with 394 tiny little hooks that, realistically, would take an hour to undo) you can yank off your sweatshirt, for effect.

> *Blaze ripped her dress off to expose her creamy white flesh in the glow of the candlelight. Across the dark room, she could still see Thor's heart thumping harder and harder in his chest. She knew he wanted her...knew this would be the night she would finally give herself to him.*
>
> *She sat down, draping herself across the fur-covered floor. Spreading her sumptuous thighs with Thor looking on, she called to him, not saying a word. Slowly, awkwardly, Thor moved his huge rock-hard body toward her. And then, in a flash, the two shadowy figures became one heaving mass.*

Notice that no one in a trashy novel is ever named Bob or Susan. They're pretty funny, but if you give them a chance, they'll help you live out fantasies you never even knew you had.

There are no rules to reading romance novels aloud. You can read the female parts while your man reads the male parts, or better yet, switch roles. Or you can trade off reading whole chapters. My guess, however, is that you probably won't be able to read much more than a chapter before the real-life Blaze (you) gets swept up by rock-solid Thor (him) and you both become engulfed in fiery passion. The very worst you can do is share a few good laughs.

48.
Another Look at Erotica

While a lot of literary erotica out there is unromantic and lacking any creativity (unless you think of torture devices as *creative*) there are some exceptions worth looking into. Some of it is beautiful and doesn't deserve being lumped in with other stuff that's just nasty and unappealing. After all, many books of the ancient Hindu, Persian, or Asian traditions would today be considered "erotica" if they didn't have historic and religious value. Even in the Bible, Song of Solomon can get pretty steamy.

Some contemporary erotica is written beautifully and just for women. When I say it's written just for women, I mean that the writer spends an extraordinary amount of time in the setup. Men reading this stuff would go crazy with impatience, wishing that the author would get to the good part already. But to women, the setup is every bit as good as the destination. To us, that's what romance *is*. The authors of some adventurous and unrestricted romantic literature understand that.

But where to find these books without having to tiptoe through back-alley shops you fear? Do I have a secret for you!

Academic or university bookstores are sensational sources when it comes to finding the best in any genre, including erotica. At your more liberal universities, erotica is considered just another worthy literary art, so they don't shy away from carefully selecting and selling great books of the genre.

It was at the University Bookstore in Seattle where I stumbled across the book *Seductions* (Plume-Penguin, 2000), edited by Lonnie Barback, Ph.D. Barback is also the editor of *Pleasures* and *Erotic Interludes: Tales Told by Women*.

A lot of people would definitely be offended by the explicit nature of the stories in *Seductions*, but all were obviously written with the female reader in mind.

Get to know your local university, college, or liberal-academic bookstore and take a look at the different kinds of romantic books they have to offer. You may find not only some of the best erotica there but also the best in love poetry and romantic collections of religious literature. You never know what you might find. It might be just the kind of thing you're looking for.

*"Pleasure is the object, the duty, and the goal
of all rational creatures."*
—Voltaire (François Marie Arouet)

We've all heard about research that claims men think of sex some ridiculous number of times a day, like 10,954. As ludicrous as all those statistics sound, there's a strong connection between the fact that men think about it more often and have an easier time getting into the mood than women.

When you look at the lives of women, it should come as no shock that women think about sex less. After all, we are the masters at prioritizing. We are efficiency *incarnate.* Not everything can be on the A list, so naturally time for daydreaming about sex falls to dead last. And why shouldn't it? We've got carpools, jobs, and the cell phone ringing like mad. We can't make everyone's problems *our* problems, carry the weight of the world on our shoulders, and solve the Mideast-side Elementary Recess Peace Crisis *and* think about our own needs, our own desires. No wonder we don't have time to think about sex!

Men are better at thinking about themselves. That's not an insult; it's a compliment. They're able to think often about the sex they'd like to have, just like they're capable of thinking about the workout they plan to squeeze in at the gym, no matter what their office or family demands may be that day. Men think about getting themselves dressed before thinking about what their children will wear. They think about what they want to eat without worrying about the sad fact that Billy is pretending to be green-vegetable intolerant. It's not that they don't care, it's just that other people's problems aren't their first concerns.

You can call men selfish for being the way they are, but they deserve some applause for taking care of their own needs. Just as a man is able to take care of all his other needs more easily than women, by putting himself first, he is also free to daydream about sex more often. Granted, with him it's more like an involuntary reflex.

For a few weeks, be like a guy. Try attending to your own needs first. Make an effort to think about sex more often. Indulge in a little daydreaming. You may be surprised how much easier it becomes to feel frisky.

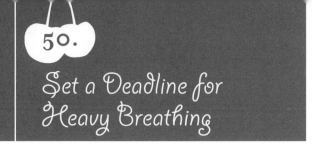

50.
Set a Deadline for Heavy Breathing

"Serving one's own passions is the greatest slavery."
—Thomas Fuller

Some couples don't have communication problems. Some couples enjoy one another's company so much that they could actually talk the night away, laughing and reminiscing until they're both much too tired to get *seriously* romantic. That's the case for lots of couples out there, and it's the case for Gary and me, too.

Most of the advice you'll ever read about reigniting romance centers on communication problems. What if communication is *too* good? One marriage counselor gave me the answer I was looking for.

I was working on a television report on the latest divorce statistics and reasons couples cite for divorcing. The counselor, whom I'd interviewed many times and whose opinions I really respect, started in with the usual lecture about a couple's need for good, honest communication.

I finally got up the nerve to ask him, "What about the couples who have *great* communication, love talking to one another, could make each other laugh until two in the morning?" Sometimes *those* couples are the ones who struggle with intimacy because they're having so much fun enjoying each other's company—they never get to the lovemaking.

It didn't take a genius to figure out that I was talking about *my marriage.* The counselor first reassured me by telling me that if all his clients were going to have marital problems, *that's* the problem he wished they had. Much easier to solve, he said. And then he offered the simplest solution I've ever heard.

"Set a deadline for heavy breathing. Have a great time with one another, but make a promise that by 10:30, *somebody* needs to be breathing heavily."

We tried it, and it works. Heavy breathing by 10:30. We can take a few hours just to talk and laugh and enjoy each other's company, but when the clock hits 10:30, we make sure we're at least starting to make more romantic overtures toward each other. You may think that putting a clock on heavy breathing takes some of the romance out of it. It doesn't. Our deadline for heavy breathing just serves as a reminder to us that while we love talking and laughing with one another, we also love many other aspects to our relationship, and they deserve time and attention, too.

51.
Foreplay Begins at Breakfast

"What I do and what I dream include thee, as the wine must taste of its own grapes."
—Elizabeth Barrett Browning

A friend shared the romance advice she considered the wisest and best she ever heard: foreplay begins in the morning with the aroma of coffee made by one partner for the other.

"When I heard that from a marriage counselor, I thought it perfectly encapsulated everything I'd been trying to express to Peter, but couldn't find the words. Foreplay isn't just the thing you do twenty minutes prior to sex. It's something that should be building all day long, and it's both people's responsibility," Josephine told me.

But how do you get your partner on board, occasionally making the coffee and building up to an evening interlude?

And how do you keep the foreplay going in the right direction all the way to nightfall? Naturally, it depends on the couple. For some, it can mean one or two phone calls just to say, "I love you" during the workday. For others, it means leaving a nice note in a briefcase, or sending a sexy email. In Josephine's case, it means thanking and praising Peter profusely for being so sweet about making the morning coffee just the way she likes it. That keeps him in a more enthusiastic mood about doing kind and romantic things throughout the day for Josephine. Praise is all the encouragement Peter needs to continue to be romantic right on through the night.

The therapist who offered the advice about having foreplay for breakfast was really saying that loving is something we should be doing all the time, not just when we want something, and certainly not just in the few minutes leading up to lovemaking. Love is something that should be brewing all day, every day of our lives. If you identify the kinds of romantic forms of expression that you really enjoy, it won't feel like work. You'll find that foreplay can actually be effortless once you expand your definition to include tiny little signs of affection.

Talk about it with your mate. Start by asking him how you could make him feel loved in the morning so that he feels like returning the favor in the evening, and listen to what he has to say. Love and romance aren't just nouns, they're active verbs. Try to make those verbs active in the morning hours, and see if they can help activate your nights, too.

52

Afternoon Amore

"We are minor in everything but our passions."
—*Elizabeth Bowen*

All Betty and Steve need to recapture romance is a few minutes together in the peace and solitude of their own beautiful home in the afternoon at least a few times each week.

In the mornings and evenings, their home is a whir of activity. Two active school-aged children keep the place buzzing with energy. Playmates let themselves in and out like they own the place. Homework and art projects demand constant attention from one or both parents. And then there are the carpools to sports teams, dance classes, and afternoon clubs. Of course, somebody's got to pay the bills and both Betty and Steve do that too, with dual careers that scream for attention day and night.

With all this going on, they tell me they'd feel like total strangers living in complete chaos if it weren't for their great afternoons of romance. Betty and Steve make time every single week to enjoy "lunch" at home together. I'm sure they actually eat, too. But that's not of primary concern. Sex isn't really a primary concern either. They use their afternoons together to reconnect, to have a conversation without the chaos of their children and career interrupting.

They talk. They sit and enjoy the quiet and the company of one another. They feel at peace together. And often, it leads to lovemaking. Being home alone makes them feel like love-struck teenagers all over again.

"I just love being home alone with Steve. It's just so nice to be together and really enjoy your own home. To have the house *quiet* and be together, free to do whatever you want without interruption," Betty tells me.

I should probably mention that Betty is also an interior decorator, and Steve is a realtor—so their home really is a place where anyone would want to spend a quiet, romantic afternoon. But without their afternoons of amore, they would never get the opportunity to enjoy the beautiful home they've created together.

Most couples would say they couldn't *possibly* meet at home for lunch once or twice a week. But Steve and Betty, busy professionals, would tell you that you always have a choice: if you *can't* meet for some kind of quiet time together, then you should really admit to yourself that you're just plain choosing not to.

You might say you can't afford the time, but Betty and Steve suggest that you can't afford *not* to find the time. This isn't to say that making love a priority doesn't have its unfortunate consequences sometimes. Betty may irk a client or two by sticking to her lunch date. Ditto for Steve. But for Betty and Steve, the point of their careers is to support their family and create a comfortable living. They recognize that the foundation of their family is their happy marriage. They've made a choice to make it number one and live with the consequences. And the consequences, they say, are delicious.

53

The Make-Out Couch

"We must act out passion before we can feel it."
—Jean-Paul Sartre

Remember all those steamy nights of your youth? Hot kisses and heavy breathing as your skin melted into the vinyl couch of his parents' basement?

Some of the most passionate moments of your life have happened on a make-out couch. Why did we ever get rid of them? OK, so they were pitifully ugly. But they don't have to be. Time to get a function-specific couch, or reappropriate one you already have.

The best place for it may be in the bedroom, so if you have limited space like most people, perhaps you should think *love seat*. How appropriate!

Here's another reason why I'm such a big fan of bringing back the make-out couch: beds are for sleeping. Sleep therapists insist beds should be used only for sleeping. They say you shouldn't read or study in bed or you'll train yourself to think of the bed as *not necessarily* just for sleeping, and insomnia could develop or worsen. It's a mystery to me why none of them talk about sex. If *reading* in bed is bad for sleep, is sex bad, too? If you get yourself so well-trained to think of the bed as being *just for slumber*, then could any sex in that bed be very good? Mightn't you get sleepy and lethargic before you even get started?

We can also learn some lessons on this from organizational counselors. Organizational counselors also train us to think in terms of "designated areas" or "zones." Dining, food preparation, beauty, reading—they're all worthy of their own designated area, and wherever that area is, all the zone-related things should be kept. For example, you wouldn't keep your rolling pin in the pantry on the other end of the kitchen, far away from your preparation zone. You'd find a way to organize all your food-prep stuff right within arm's reach of the food-prep area.

When you look at it this way, hundreds of task-specific areas comprise the whole house. Many of us already use this organizational approach; we just don't realize it, and probably don't use it to it's maximum potential.

If every place has a zone, it seems to me that we need a part of the bedroom to serve as a "sex zone!" I think that zone should include a make-out couch or love seat. It's more comfortable than having a sectioned off area of the carpet as the "sex zone," in my book. That's not to say that you couldn't take what has *begun* in the "sex zone" and casually continue it over in the "sleeping zone." There are no zone police, as far as I know.

You may think I'm going a little nuts on the zone theory, but let me give you another reason for it. I once met a very earthy couple who tried to help me learn how to meditate. Part of their meditation routine was astral projection. They could get to an altered state of consciousness very easily, and they also had frequent out-of-body experiences and other metaphysical adventures that sounded really cool to me. What was their secret? They said they had a meditation couch, a couch they only used for meditating and out-of-body experiences. They said that because they had started the habit of using that particular couch in that way, whenever they sat down on that couch; their body and mind were programmed to *go*.

Their couch was their magic carpet of sorts, only there was nothing magical about the couch. They had just trained their minds, bodies, and spirits that whenever they sat down there, it was liftoff time. In fact, they said if they tried to use the couch in another way, they would *still* lift off. They had themselves so well trained they couldn't help but do what they were supposed to do on *that* couch.

Imagine the implications of a make-out love seat in your bedroom. You *know* what it's there for. Imagine just sitting on it and suddenly feeling hot and bothered. Since busy women tend to have a difficult time relaxing and getting in the mood, couldn't this be a great tool? If you used it often, you could actually train yourself to get in the mood quickly, even if romance is the last thing on your mind before you sit down.

Best of all, it doesn't have to be exactly like the make-out couches of your high-school days. Mercifully, it doesn't have to be puke-green vinyl. It doesn't have to have a crocheted afghan in orange, green, and brown draped across the back. It doesn't have to be in a dark, musty basement. And you don't have to jump six feet in the air in panic if you hear a car pulling into the driveway, signaling that his parents have come home, although at least one of my friends swears that's half the appeal: knowing that you're doing something you're not supposed to and could be caught doing at any moment. In that case, go ahead and jump.

Designate a make-out couch and see what happens!

54.
Learn To Belly Dance

"Dancing is the loftiest, the most moving, the most beautiful of the arts, because it is no mere translation or abstraction from life; it is life itself."
—Havelock Ellis

Many women are living lives above the neck, disconnected from their bodies. We live in our minds and deny the existence of our beautiful feminine forms. We divorce ourselves from our body's romantic nature and its natural expressiveness.

Perhaps in our efforts to be taken seriously for what's going on in our heads and not just objectified because of the shapeliness of our bodies, we've forgotten that our bodies have great value, intelligence, and spirituality—qualities that we should be really proud of. But we've lost touch with our bodies. We've stopped communicating with them. We've forgotten why they're so beautiful.

There are a lot of ways to shift our thinking, and one great way is to reconnect through dance, specifically the belly or hula dance. They are ancient arts that celebrate women for their natural, curvy feminine forms.

Both dances have become tremendously popular, with women turning to the Middle Eastern art of belly dance like never before.

Delilah, a celebrated belly-dance instructor and lecturer in Seattle, understands. She teaches women from preteens to their eighties that beauty is not a noun, but rather a verb. Beauty is something our bodies want to express through dance, and it's something women of all backgrounds, ethnicities, and sizes can celebrate. She insists that a woman's body has stories to tell that celebrate life, the history of womanhood, and all creation.

"Belly dancing is earthy; it's visceral. There's a mystery and hypnotic aspect to it. It's also liberating because we're saying that we have a right to move our hips and our breasts," says Delilah.

Since many women first come to Delilah's class hating their bodies, the most important first steps of learning the dance include healing and self-discovery. Eventually they learn to love their bodies and appreciate all the amazing things they're able to do. A woman's body holds all the mysteries of life.

"There's a healing going on when we dance—deep soul work, accepting yourself, your body. Our bodies can tell stories of life, stories that are beautiful, tender, painful—it's the story of life and it goes way deeper than choreography."

Delilah says women come to belly dance for many reasons. Some come to the dance already strong and independent, but there are others who are timid and shy, and she says the transformation that happens as they learn the dance is amazing.

"Once women start dancing, their lives start changing. You start liberating your body and your life; changes start happening. Once this movement begins, it starts something and she becomes a different person."

Delilah also says she gets a lot of students who are older women, looking for a way to still feel beautiful even though there's no proof in magazines or movies that women over a certain age still belong in the world of beauty.

"I've seen it revitalize the romance in marriages. This more mature woman learns how to dance and be beautiful, and one day her husband looks up from his newspaper and says, 'Wow! Who's this?'"

In short, belly dance can help us get our groove back, something we may have lost for a variety of reasons. Some women come to Delilah after working in a male-dominated business world that forces them to cut themselves off from their womanhood. Other women come in search of connection when their bodies and minds are tired, trying to meet the daily demands of motherhood. Delilah asks women to give the movement a chance and, through the dance, become reacquainted with their bodies.

"The minute we cut ourselves off from that [our bodies], then we don't want to have sex anymore. We start to isolate ourselves. We are, in fact, in mourning.

"Who feels like sex if they don't feel pretty? Belly dance helps women feel beautiful by helping them reconnect with that fuse, that life force inside us. By moving your body and feeling your body, you make yourself feel treasured, treasuring that life force inside you."

If you're feeling disconnected from your body, if you rarely move it in a way that you'd consider sensual or artistic, consider giving something like hula or belly dance a try. It may be scary at first. You may feel ridiculous. Delilah says that a lot of women come to class thinking, *Well, this will be a fun little lark.*

But she says their reasons for coming back change rapidly. Pretty soon they're connecting with body and spirit sensations that are either completely new or that they thought they had lost forever. It's pretty powerful stuff that may contain the secret to romance you're searching for.

"The voice is a second face."
—Gerard Bauer

*I*t's said that when you really want to say something important, *whisper.*

When she became America's first lady, Jacqueline Kennedy mesmerized a country but confounded journalists. They didn't know what to make of this vision of beauty who was obviously quite intelligent and well educated. They weren't bewildered by those qualities; it was the fact that she had those qualities and still spoke at a volume that dogs could barely hear. She spoke quietly, almost at a whisper.

Some journalists criticized her for speaking so quietly, almost like a little girl, they would say. Others recognized her brilliance immediately: talking very quietly forces others to lean in and listen very attentively. She forced them to hang on her every word. They were fixated and hypnotized by her soft voice and gentle words. When Jackie spoke, you could hear a pin drop on the marble floors of the White House.

It also worked its magic in impressing one of American history's sexiest men of power *ever*, not to mention generations of Americans who hold her up as a legend, an icon of femininity.

We can all take a lesson from her and learn how to make men listen to us—*really* listen to us—by speaking softly. Not necessarily all the time. Just when we have something really important to say.

How would you rather hear your lover say, "I love you": in a normal tone? Or whispered, looking straight into your eyes, feeling the words brush across your face?

Whispering is a great way to tell your partner, *Listen to me, what I'm about to say is more important than anything I've said to you all week.* Speaking softly forces him to lean in and listen with both ears and his whole mind. There's no doubt that speaking softly is more captivating, more intriguing, more romantic.

It also has more power. Forget the myth that speaking loudly conveys power. Remember Jackie. Remember Grace Kelly. Think of Audrey Hepburn. They're all women who wielded tremendous power but often spoke in little more than a whisper. Discover the power and romance of the softly spoken word.

56.

Public Displays of Affection

"The important thing is being capable of emotions, but to experience only one's own would be a sorry limitation."
—André Gide

My simple philosophy is this: If you take public displays of affection away from responsible adults, public displays of affection will only be in the hands of irresponsible teenagers.

Public displays of affection. We've all grown up to be so respectful and responsible the state could almost build a two-lane highway between you and your date on any given night. Where's the love?

Why should teenagers be the only ones to enjoy the fun and freedom of kissing (even making out) in public? I'm not saying I've always been a huge fan of public displays of affection. But eventually, I realized that the rules against it were only being obeyed by those of us in mature, monogamous, loving relationships. I ask you, is that right?

If some people are inevitably going to break the unwritten rule against public displays of affection, why should it be the people who are in fly-by-night relationships with dates whose names they can't even remember? Why shouldn't the rule-breaking be afforded to the people who are following all of society's other rules?

Why shouldn't the public displays of affection rule-breakers be grandparents who've *earned* the right to make out in public if they feel like it? They've been together for fifty-seven years, through good times and bad.

They should be lovey-dovey where all can see them so they can teach the rest of us how to make love last a lifetime.

I'm not suggesting that you start making out with your mate at some church potluck. How weird would that be? But will the walls of the church collapse and the sanctity of the sanctuary melt away if you dared to give each other *a kiss?*

So here's what I propose: humiliate the teenagers in your life by kissing in public with the one that you love. Show them what true love is. Hold hands and wrap your arms around each other. Nuzzle. Look into each other's eyes and just stare until the bare-midriffed teenagers are mortified. Change the world with everlasting love!

57.
Make Love Under the Stars

"Nature knows no indecencies; man invents them."
—Mark Twain

Remember when you were a kid, and camping out in the backyard seemed almost as good as camping out for real in the wilderness?

My friends and cousins and I used to love sleeping in the backyard. Somehow it seemed like such an adventure, even though we were maybe twenty whole feet away from the kitchen and conveniences of indoor plumbing.

As kids we never thought about the ground being hard and the air being damp. We never worried about bug bites or the weather forecast. We just plopped our sleeping bags down on the lawn and gazed at the stars, telling ghost stories and pretending to hear the sounds of wild animals (in the *suburbs*). If it started raining in the middle of the night (in Seattle, it seemed like it *always* did), we'd just run inside and resume our campout on the floor of the living room.

How and when did a little adventure like sleeping under the stars in the backyard become so complicated? Does it slip away so slowly you don't even notice until it's completely gone? Does that sense of everyday adventure just vanish on a particular birthday?

Grab a sleeping bag and a lover (okay, *and* an air mattress or foam padding to avoid an emergency trip to the chiropractor) and camp out in your back yard!

Make love under the stars. Bring your flashlight and read scary stories aloud. Watch the bats in action (easiest when there's a full moon). Bring popcorn or snacks and bottled water.

Identify the Big and Little Dippers. Find Cassiopeia. Talk about what you would do with a million-trillion-zillion dollars. Talk about what you want to be when you grow up. Don't let the conversation drift into boring, stressful adult talk.

Hold hands. Dream big together, under the stars. Make love again.

It may rain. It may not. Be like a kid and don't let the forecast or any other kind of "adult thinking" stop you.

Camping in the backyard is like taking a vacation from all adult thinking. And we all know that vacations can work miracles in terms of freeing your mind from stresses and clearing room in your life for wonderful romance.

58.

Make Out In the Car Wash

"Wickedness is a myth invented by good people to account for the curious attractiveness of others."
—Oscar Wilde

The average drive-through car wash takes, what, six minutes to complete? You don't have time to do much else; there's no adequate lighting for reading. Talking is *highly overrated*. So that leaves kissing!

You can make the most of your car wash kissing by:

- Remembering to bring your kissing partner with you to the car wash. (More difficult than it sounds if your car *really does* need washing).
- Off-roading more often so your car needs washing.
- Ordering the car-wash package that includes *auto-waxing* (it makes the ride last longer).
- Having lip balm handy and a great CD already playing.
- Doing your homework to find the car wash in your area that takes the longest with the fewest attendants.

Of course, after six to eight minutes of kissing, you won't want to stop. So try to time your car washes so that you can spend some quality romantic time together afterward.

The car wash is the perfect remedy for the woman who complains that there's not enough kissing anymore and the partner who doesn't seem to get the message. A car wash is a great place to do some serious kissing because you don't have the time or the freedom of movement to really progress too much *beyond* the simple kiss.

Eight minutes later, he's now interested in something much more serious than kissing, and you're likely to be open to the idea.

59.
Code Cracking

The happiest, most romantic couples I know all have their own code languages that they use to communicate to each other in any situation, at any time.

One friend tells me the code language she and her husband use has proved invaluable at dinner and cocktail parties, family gatherings, and any other situation when other people are around or talking is prohibited (like a movie theater). All Ellen has to do at a party is start talking about how much she's always wanted to travel to Macchu Pichu, and Bill knows it's time to save her from a boring or otherwise unpleasant conversation.

One word used strangely, like "sunshine," or a gesture subtly made, like toying with an earring or dropping a pen, signals a secret command to the other partner.

Try using a code and you may find that it's a cool, fun, sexy tool in the mission to bring more romance into your life. Once you've made the obligatory appearance at an office party, you can find the right moment to send out the secret signal that means, "Let's get out of here; I can't wait another minute to be alone with you." You can also choreograph a signal that means, "Let's find a quiet, private place to be together."

Ellen says she and her husband have also used the code to protect each other from predators. It's not uncommon for people to make the moves on the partners in this fun, good-looking couple. Ellen has a sneezing attack and Bill knows to come save her from some leech. Bill drops an hors d'oeuvre on the floor and Ellen knows it's time to come running.

Around relatives, codes can be especially helpful. A kiss on the cheek reminds a partner not to let an opinionated, overbearing, intrusive relative get the best of him. A wink says, "I love you."

Best of all, codes are sworn secrets, and every romantic couple should have a few secrets of their own. Secrets keep us close. They remind us that we're on the same team. They keep us on the same wavelength and reinforce communication that actually *works*. Codes keep us attentive and watchful. After all, you have to be on your toes to notice your lover subtly tugging on his earlobe or bringing up the horrible annoyance of "static cling."

60.
Tinker with the Thermostat

*"What men call gallantry, and gods adultery,
Is much more common where the climate's sultry."*
—Lord Byron

A friend of mine, I'll call him "Dave" (since that's his real name), came up with this idea on his own. He keeps the temperature in his home somewhere in the 99 degree range. His wife often complains. He tells her if it's too hot, she can simply remove some clothing. She grumbles, but soon enough she's walking around the house, shedding clothing as she goes. In Dave's own pursuit of romance, this makes him think, *Woo-hoo, mission almost accomplished!*

I'm not sure Dave's idea is the most environmentally sensitive way to fire up the romance, but it seems to work for him.

I have a better idea: turn the heat down at night. Way down. If you have kids, get them heavy wool blankets to keep them warm. But keep your own comforter as is. This is called getting close the old-fashioned way.

If you were ever unlucky enough to hear some of the tales from your grandparents or great-grandparents on the subject of romance, they probably shared that, in the olden days, a winter cold snap meant a baby's cry come September. Our great-grandparents didn't have electric blankets or super-insulated vinyl windows that kept the heat in. They were forced to keep the romance alive to keep each other alive some nights. I'm grateful for many of the modern-day conveniences, but in some ways, things have become too convenient.

Try turning down the heat and turning up the passion.

61.
Sleep in the Buff

veryone has a different theory on this one. Wacky comedic genius Phyllis Diller wrote and often said that a woman should wear something skimpy and appealing when she comes to bed—even if she has to buy that skimpy something in a size fifty-two. There's some powerful truth in that joke.

But once you tinker with the thermostat, you'll be tempted to continue just wearing the sweats, socks, and flannel shirt that may have become your nighttime uniform over the years. Don't.

It's a well-known fact that two naked bodies together produce more heat than two individuals sleeping side by side, fully clothed. Naked is good.

If you happen to enjoy lingerie, you should know that according to a survey published in *Redbook*'s *Married Lust*, the greatest number of husbands polled would be most turned on by seeing their wives in a black bustier and black garter. A sizable number of men also liked the idea of a plunging red lace bra and matching thong. In a close third place was a creamy colored silk teddy and tap shorts. Practically no men at all were turned on by the idea of a simple white bra and briefs (damn!). I guess familiarity really does breed contempt.

But the above research has very little to do with what you should actually be *sleeping* in, which is—nothing at all. Sleeping in the buff is a very good hygiene practice. We need air down there. And men who wear loose clothing or nothing to bed are more fertile (a good or bad thing, depending on where you are in life).

Sleeping in the buff will automatically create more intimate moments.

62

Early-Morning Romance

"Take away all from me, but leave me Ecstasy."
—Emily Dickinson

Early-morning romance can be the *best* kind of romance. Picture the sun rising, peeking over the horizon. Hear and smell the coffee brewing in the kitchen. And meanwhile, you're brewing something special of your own.

There are lots of reasons why many couples claim that morning romance is the best romance. At the end of the day, you're often exhausted and you just want to fall into bed at the earliest opportunity. Romance is likely the last thing on your mind. There are many reasons why you need to go to bed earlier anyway, and early-morning romance tops the list of reasons.

After a good night's sleep, you'll discover that you have so much more energy for talking, cuddling, and romancing than you could have possibly mustered even in the early evening at the end of a very long day.

Set your alarm an hour earlier and make way for romance in the morning. Light some candles. Play some wonderful music. Watch the sun rise while cuddling together.

The other fantastic benefit if you're a parent is that you'll never be able to get the kids settled in bed early enough in the evening to have the time and the energy to devote your full attention to even a few romantic minutes.

At the crack of dawn, unless you have a newborn baby, there's no battle for your attentions or affections. The children are usually fast asleep,
and the phone had better not be ringing. You're awake, you're refreshed,
and you're ready for romance.

63

Upgrade Your Undies

"From the cradle to the coffin, underwear comes first."
—Bertolt Brecht

Y ou'd like to feel more romantic, and you'd love more spontaneous love in your life. But when it happens, do you really want to be caught wearing *those* underthings?

A friend of mine, Melissa, who happens to be a high-earning businesswoman who can more than afford nice things, confessed to me that she recently went through her underwear drawer and was disgusted by what she found. They were the exact same garments she wore every day, but she finally saw them for what they really were: hideous.

We laughed as she described the awful truth about them.

"They could almost be described as 'ratty'!" she told me. "I held up my bras, and I thought, *This is pathetic. These aren't even remotely attractive.*"

Melissa promptly went to Nordstrom and upgraded.

We had a good laugh about how such an everyday necessity as underwear falls to last on the list for a busy mom who would never, ever let her husband or kids walk around in underwear that looked that bad.

Why is it that we lower our standards when it comes to ourselves?

Part of the issue can best be explained by my husband, who believes that it takes a good five years for a pair of underwear to *start* to get comfortable. To him, they're like old friends, too easygoing to ever part with.

According to my husband, underwear starts hitting its prime at about ten years. But I have a confession to make. He only *thinks* he's wearing ten-year-old underwear. They rarely make it to four years old before I sneak them into the trash. He thinks our dryer eats them.

I've always admired women who wear matching bras and panties and seem to have a silky, neverending, colorful supply. They seem, as I glance their way in the locker room at the gym, to enjoy those nearly naked moments. They show off their undies. Meanwhile, the rest of us are in a frantic race against time and the last threads of our underwear to switch from outfit to outfit at breakneck speed—praying that the people with pretty underwear are too intoxicated by their own beauty to cast a wayward glance our way.

Sometimes we think pretty, matching panties and undies are a waste of money and fabric unless our bodies match our ideals of physical perfection. We are tainted by the advertising world's vision of perfection. Fortunately, men aren't so easily tainted. They continue to love the female form with all its curves and excesses with no regard to the latest images of anorexic models in the popular magazines. Here's a place where we could learn something from men when it comes to romance. Our bodies are romantic, as curvaceous and "un-ideal" as they may be. We should wrap them in pretty things no matter what our size or shape is—or once was—and might someday be again.

Melissa's revelation and reaction inspired me. *No more ugly underwear!*

I've made this decision, and you should too. They don't have to be silky; they don't have to be colorful; they needn't be expensive; it would be *nice* if they were matching; but they *must* be attractive.

"Honest to God, it changes the way you carry yourself, knowing that you're wearing something attractive underneath," says Melissa.

Pledge with me now that you will henceforth wear attractive underwear. You're bound to feel sexier and more romantic knowing that you're wearing something pretty. Not necessarily *raunchy.* Not necessarily lacy. Not necessarily frou-frou, or *hot,* or even sexy, but at least pretty. You deserve it.

64.
Do Like John and Yoko

"Rituals are important. Nowadays it's hip not to be married. I'm not interested in being hip."

—John Lennon

One of the really interesting things that became a ritual for John Lennon and Yoko Ono was to hold "bed-ins" at various hotels around the world, protesting war. Lennon said rather than go to cities and run around holding press conferences at various places, it was easier just to stay in his hotel room bed and invite the media to his suite. It was also a brilliant ploy in guaranteeing the media's attention.

You don't have to be taking a stand on politics or holding a news conference to enjoy a good old-fashioned bed-in and make it a ritual of your own. Just check into a nice hotel and spend forty-eight hours or more in bed, getting up only for the restroom and room service.

You could hold your own bed-in at your own home, but I really think John and Yoko had it right by staying in fabulous hotels instead.

There are so many reasons why I think holding a bed-in is such a great idea. There's the obvious: that you'll end up making love dozens of times. You'll catch up on your sleep and reading. You're guaranteed hours of relaxation. And then there are the less obvious reasons, like really taking the time to enjoy the expensive hotel room you paid for.

Have you ever stayed in a sensational hotel only to end up leaving feeling like you didn't really take full advantage of your lush room? Did you treat it like a place to dump your stuff and change clothes before rushing off to the next great sightseeing destination? If you're staying at an inn or hotel that's truly wonderful, why not get the full experience by staying in your room like honeymooners?

For that reason, you should probably hold your bed-in at a wonderful hotel within fifteen minutes of home. You've already seen the sights your hometown has to offer. Staying *in* your deluxe room will, in this case, be the best way to get your money's worth.

For your bed-in, you'll want to bring reading material (I recommend trashy novels) and sexy food you won't get from room service (grapes?). You may want to bring massage oil or a nail kit. Yes, this is the perfect time to give each other deluxe manicures and pedicures.

Allot some extra money for Pay-Per-View. Catch up on all the movies you haven't had time to see lately.

Another great thing about a bed-in is that you can pack *really* light. Like your toothbrush and that's it. You won't need any extra clothing. None. No makeup. No extra shoes. Just the outfit you're wearing and a credit card.

You may never experience anything so relaxing as a wonderful room, no place to go, and nothing to wear even if you should get an impulse.

A bed-in can be really romantic. And just think, finally *you'll be* the people behind the mysterious door with the *Do Not Disturb* sign hanging from the doorknob for three days straight. You'll be the talk of the housekeeping and room service staff, if not the whole hotel. People will toast to your couplehood when you finally reemerge. They'll look at you like you're Hugh Hefner and Pamela Anderson. OK, perhaps not, but you can *pretend* they're all staring at you, whispering about the lovebirds of the ninth floor.

You can relive one of the original Lennon/Ono bed-ins yourself by staying at the Fairmont The Queen Elizabeth Hotel in Montreal. You can even request the same suite. The hotel offers bed-in packages that include a souvenir photo of the 1969 event, breakfast for two, a bottle of sparkling wine, and a welcome gift.

65.

Become a Romance Voyeur

"Love rules the court, the camp, the grove,
the men below, and the saints above;
For love is heaven, and heaven is love."
—Sir Walter Scott

You know you've become detached from your romantic self when you start to despise those cute couples holding hands and smooching in your neighborhood park. If it's all that you can do to resist yelling, "Get a room!" it's time to step back and take a good long look at what's happened to your romantic nature.

Whether you're in a relationship or not, struggling to rekindle romance in your relationship, or even if you are already swimming in passion—you can still look to strangers in love and get a momentary sense of romance.

Some afternoon, grab a latte and park yourself on a park bench. Focus on the happy people going by. Watch the couples soaking up the sun on a blanket, kissing each other, and feel their love. When you see an older couple walking by, arm in arm, smiling at each other, bring their love into your heart and send it back out again. Feel the romance all around you.

If you're doing it right, you should faintly hear the song "What A Wonderful World" playing in the background. There *is* love all around us. There is romance to be enjoyed everywhere. If we don't see it, it's our own fault.

It's our fault if we're too focused on war and rampant divorce and rising road rage. In spite of the prevalence of all those things, there are still long-married couples enjoying a kiss. There are still young lovers who can barely keep their hands off each other as the dance of nature takes over. There are mothers stroking the faces of sleeping babies in strollers and fathers teaching their kids to play catch. There are men carrying flowers home. There are promises of forever being made—and kept. There are butterfly and Eskimo kisses going on all around us if we just open our eyes to them.

Take the time to sit down, breathe deeply, and watch the romance all around you. It's heartwarming and inspiring. It makes you feel better about the state of the world. It will bring you closer to God and to the one you love. Becoming a romance voyeur will make you feel gratitude for all the wonderful things you have and the opportunity you have every day to give a meaningful kiss and to look into someone's eyes like you never want the moment to end.

66.

Erotic Dishwashing

"Pleasant words are the food of love."
—Ovid

Towering suds. Hot soapy water. A lemon-fresh scent. The kids, sensing the onset of a domestic chore, have long disappeared, escaping silently into their rooms. The two of you. There. Alone. Just a sink and elbow-high yellow gloves standing between you and erotic bliss. What more could you possibly ask from a scene with romantic potential?

Dishwashing together can be highly passionate, depending on how creative you are and how determined you are to get the dishes washed in a timely fashion. The same is true for vacuuming, shower scrubbing, floor washing, sheet changing, and anything else domestic besides taking out the trash and getting the mail (though these, too, *could* be romantic—I'm just not sure how).

There are opportunities all around us to make the ordinary moments in our lives at home extraordinarily romantic. After all, isn't one of our quests to find steamy opportunities outside of the more obvious *Saturday night, lights out*? Who says extraordinary romance has to involve a hotel room or even a locked bedroom door?

There are things we all must do every single day to make our living space habitable and to keep our household running. Why not make some of them a little more fun and adventurous? Put Palmolive dishwashing liquid to the test. Does it *really* soften skin while dissolving baked-on, caked-on dirty pans? At the very least, you could do some quality kissing in the kitchen.

The point is—take everyday activities and make them more romantic. This is the ultimate solution for couples who complain there's just no time for passion anymore. There is time if you're willing to multitask.

And there's something else to be said about domestic life here. Relationship researchers have found that it's not just the mad, passionate moments in our lives that are most telling about the level of intimacy and our chances for making the relationship work. Little chores performed together can be the most revealing. Those moments are the times that relationship researcher John Gottman, Ph.D., (author of *The Seven Principles For Making Marriage Work)* watches like a hawk in his search for clues about how a relationship is really doing.

In a research lab Gottman transformed into an apartment, he watches a couple go about daily life. And what he looks for is pretty surprising. As the couple proceeds with routine chores or daily activities like reading the newspaper or washing dishes, Gottman watches to see if the couple operates independently or if they include each other in tiny, seemingly insignificant ways. Does the husband comment to the wife about some article he's reading? If he does, does she respond to or ignore him? Does the husband unceremoniously join in with the dishwashing? The more interactions like this, the better the health of the relationship, according to Gottman, even if the interaction includes some bickering. It's the interconnectedness that's critical.

So don't ignore the amazing potential that household chores and routine tasks hold for the vitality of your relationship and romance. Even if you don't take my advice to make dishwashing more erotic or sweeping more sexy, recognize that it's important that you not shut each other out while going about the little things that swallow up the majority of our time at home. The interaction can be erotic, consist of monosyllabic comments, or be silent but helpful (like his moving the coffee table when he notices you're vacuuming). Any of the above can keep a relationship rich in romance and happiness.

Look for opportunities to connect. And the next time you find yourself loading the dishwasher together, don't worry about the fact that he's putting the plastic on the bottom where it will melt. He may be ruining the Tupperware, but he's helping your relationship.

67.
Indulge in Fantasy

*"Few have greater riches than the joy
That comes to us in visions,
In dreams which nobody can take away."*
—Euripides

We all fantasize, dream little dreams about some ideal physical specimen of a man (or woman) sweeping us off our feet and carrying us away to perfect rapture. Not only is fantasy healthy, but the experts say we can use it in ways to enhance our relationships.

Sex therapist Dr. Joy Davidson, contributor to *Men's Fitness* magazine and author of books on sexuality such as *How to Be a Babe*, tells me that women should stop being afraid of fantasy and find more time to indulge.

"Fantasy is poetry for the erotic soul. It's part of our healthy dream life, a source of wonderment and beauty. Fantasy inspires us, moves us creatively, and takes our sexuality beyond the ordinary," says Dr. Joy.

Should we worry when our fantasies involve movie stars, soap stars, or random men we see on the street—to the exclusion of our mates? Of course not, but Dr. Joy says if *all* your fantasies exclude your partner, it's time to look at whether you're in a sexual and fantasy rut.

"Imagine doing things with your partner that would seem out of the ordinary, even scary in real life: bondage, forcing your honey to be your sex slave, having sex on the front lawn with all the neighbors watching. The possibilities are endless."

By breaking out of the fantasy rut, Dr. Joy explains that you can enhance real-life lovemaking with your partner.

"Women who frequently fantasize have richer, more varied sex lives and are even more orgasmic than women who don't fantasize much."

The key to great fantasy life seems to be balance. You can't live solely in a fantasy world, and Dr. Joy says that if you get to the point where you'd rather spend time fantasizing alone instead of making love with your mate, it's time to take a hard look at the relationship and whether the intimacy needs some intensive care. On the other hand, when you have a healthy sexual relationship with your partner, taking regular alone time for fantasy is a wonderful enhancement.

Dr. Joy says taking time to fantasize isn't just about the wild, erotic visions of passion; it's about taking a little time to nurture your soul.

"It's important to take time just for your yourself. Our erotic life is private, personal—it's our own. We share our erotic selves with our partners, but we can't rely on them to bestow our sexuality upon us. We have to own the power of our sexuality and remind ourselves consistently that we bring a huge capacity for sexual pleasure to the relationship, not the other way around."

Take a private, honest look at whether your fantasy life is flourishing or whether you're slowly starving yourself of the kind of creative erotic pleasures that could give your spirit wings and your relationship greater passion and intensity.

We've all heard that fantasy is healthy, normal, and important. But many of us still deny ourselves the time we need to indulge. Consider expanding your ten-second daydream to a half hour of blissful self indulgence. Take time for yourself and enjoy the fantasy!

section four

the science
of romance

68.

Don't Wash

"A woman smells well when she smells of nothing."
—Plautus

apoleon once wrote to his beloved Josephine, "Home in three days. Don't wash."

I'm suggesting that you *do* try this at home. Spend an entire weekend together, *not washing*.

I know, it almost sounds like a sacrilege in our super-clean society to even suggest for a moment that we not lather up, head to toe, every single day with antibacterial, bleach-enhanced soap—then rinse and repeat. But try to imagine that in some cultures, even today, the smell of a person's sweat (especially that of a person you find attractive) is considered highly erotic.

Even in high society, at various points in history, a person's particular body odor was considered sensual and very sexy. True, back then baths weren't as easy to take and were considered to be more like an annual event. But a lover's unwashed body being sexy is something we can now prove is true.

It's rooted in science, but it's also something the makers of antiperspirants and deodorant soaps don't want you to think about too much. Sweat is sexy. Your personal smell sends out a signal to your lover. But society teaches us to hate our own scent, to despise our own bodies, to fight nature at every opportunity.

Regular bathing certainly has its place—like when we want to blend in with the crowd. It makes good sense that we should disguise the secretions of our apocrine glands while we're at work or at a social event. But why at home? Why not let our lovers smell who we are, naturally? Is it really so offensive?

It's also well documented that women have a keener sense of smell than men, even more so during ovulation. So consider asking him to refrain from using deodorants and antiperspirants while at home one weekend. Skip the perfume and aftershaves too. Skip anything that masks your scent. You'll be amazed how many products we subscribe to that are intended to do just that. (But *do* brush your teeth. I've found nothing that would indicate that minty fresh breath and gleaming white teeth ever hurt in the romance department).

You and your lover were drawn together partly because of your chemistry. A key part of your sexual chemistry is based on the compatibility of your pheromones. Why work so hard to mask one of the raw, animal factors that drew you close?

Inhale each other everywhere—all those places you're embarrassed of, thanks to product makers. It's a deeply intimate and exciting thing to do, and these are smells you'll likely enjoy and remember forever. No perfume can imitate you. Let him discover who you really are on a primal level.

Let your scent waft through the air and let nature take its course!

69.

Color Me Romantic

"O, my love is like a red, red, rose."
—Robert Burns

If the romance just isn't happening, or isn't happening as often as you'd like, maybe it isn't something you're doing wrong. Maybe there are subtle forces working against you, like the colors you're surrounded by. Sound far-fetched? Maybe, but there's plenty of research to indicate that color has a great effect on romantic feelings, and we can use this information to get in the mood—whether we're dressing or decorating our boudoirs.

Psychologists who work in the area of color psychology agree that red, the traditional Western color of romance, is an aggravating color. Feng shui experts assert that red is a great color for a room where you want to attract "chi," or life force, but color psychologists would say that it's best as an accent color.

Red rooms are known to make people feel anxious and lose track of time, and the color red stimulates one's appetite—that's why restaurants and bars like the color so much. Red definitely attracts attention, but it may also invite confrontation.

Various polls suggest that a lot of men love red lingerie on women. But one thing we should consider and question is whether a man needs the same colors as a woman to aid in achieving the mood. I suspect not. Based on what is known about men's preferences and color psychology, it may be that you should drape yourself in certain colors (like red) *for him*, but surround yourself with entirely different colors that are more romantically appealing to you.

Unless you are going to be staring in a mirror all night, it may not matter to you what color you're wearing. You can go ahead and wear the "irritating" color of red. "Irritated" could also be interpreted as "hot and bothered." Nothing wrong with that!

But you may not want to paint your bedroom in bright, vivid red—unless you just *love* the color. Women generally have a tougher time getting relaxed enough to start feeling romantic, and red is anything but relaxing. While pink will relax women, it has proven to have an emasculating effect on men. Bad for romance.

So what choices are you left with when it comes to decorating your home's most romantic rooms? Orange is out—too close to red. Blue is out, unfortunately, because while it is cooling and relaxing, studies show that it can make you depressed and tired after ten minutes of exposure to the color. White, like picket-fence white, is reported to cause headaches. Not good. Those having been eliminated, it seems the best, safest colors for a bedroom or other romantic room are warm yellow, cool green, or passionate purple.

Purple is believed to improve circulation and has a stimulating, but not aggravating, effect. Purple is a perfect mixture of red and blue, so it has the excitement of red, but the cooling, tonic quality of blue. Purple in the bedroom, if you can find a shade you can live with, could mean intense passion without hostility, depression, or tiredness. As a bonus, when you *are* ready to sleep, purple will help you. It's very restful and reportedly helps lower blood pressure.

If changing the color of your bedroom walls seems extreme, many experts in holistic healing believe that you can accomplish your goals easily through accent colors or even just candles of a particular color. Try red, pink, or orange candles, purple throws or pillows, and see how the judicious use of color can work in your favor and enhance your romantic life.

70

The Scent of Love

*"How strange are the tricks of memory, which, often
hazy as a dream about the most important events of a
man's life, religiously preserve the merest trifles."*
—Sir Richard Burton

f you've read the chapter on not washing for romantic effect,
note that this is *not* a contradictory chapter. You have to wash
sometimes and when you do get all gussied up and go out with your mate,
you should wear a tiny amount of a perfume that *means and says something*. What it should say is, *Remember when we fell in love?*

If you wore Shalimar when you were dating and fell in love, you should
be wearing Shalimar today for all your important and romantic dates.

It exasperates scientists how little they understand about how our
olfactory system works, but one thing they do know is that if you experience a powerful moment and inhale a particular scent at the time, a distinct part of the brain will remember that smell forever. Even if you only
smell it once!

Reports from the Howard Hughes Medical Institute explain that we
remember smell because the scents literally attach themselves to receptors and then travel to a particular part of the brain. This is why we can
remember a smell sixty years later, even though olfactory neurons only
have a life span of about sixty days. Now they know a part of our brain
catches, and hangs on to, scents we pick up throughout our lives.

We remember special smells forever, and they can invoke very powerful feelings. My friend Jean swears that she can spot the scent of one particular men's cologne from a half mile away, all because of a lover who wore it fifteen years ago. That's how powerful those memories connected to scent are.

We can use scent to drive our partners wild, and the best part is that person can be totally clueless as to what we're doing. He is probably not going to consciously remember the scent of a particular lotion you wore when you were first falling in love. He's just going to feel a shudder as he's carried back to another time and place when he smelled that smell. He may wrack his brain trying to figure out what is "bugging" him. Or he may not. He may just think, *Hey, something's familiar here, and I like it!* And he's going to be aroused.

The other part that I love about this is that neither of you needs to figure it out for it to be effective in reigniting romance. You may not even recognize that he's reintroduced a fragrance he used to use, but a little place in your brain *will* remember. And that little place will send signals to the rest of your body.

71

Eat Chocolate Naked

*"Without the spice of guilt,
sin cannot be fully savored."*
—Alexander Chase

You've probably heard news reports of chocolate being hailed by researchers as a bona fide aphrodisiac, only to have other scientists and nutritionists refute it, only to hear it affirmed in the news once again.

What's the truth? Women hardly need scientists to tell them. Chocolate is a feel-good food. Good feelings enhance the likelihood for romance.

The only problem with chocolate is that women *tend* to eat it when men are not around. And then when the men do come around, the women—feeling very satisfied because of the chocolate—may be less likely to pursue romance: "Who needs you? I just had chocolate!"

But if we want the good feelings of chocolate *and* the bonus of great romance, there is a solution based in science. Eat chocolate with your lover.

There actually is research that suggests that the mood-enhancing chemicals (released or triggered by eating chocolate) can be very effective in sparking our attraction for a mate—*when* said mate is present at the time of chemical release (or chocolate consumption). Translation: eat chocolate *when he's with you*.

Chocolate contains phenylethylamine (PEA) which triggers the release of chemicals our bodies produce like tryptophan, dopamine, and serotonin. Dopamine, which makes you feel somewhat "dopey" and happy, in turn triggers what's known as the "cuddle chemical," oxytocin.

No wonder we love chocolate! All these mood-enhancing chemicals and neurotransmitters are the key things we seek in life once the basics of food and shelter are covered.

If you eat chocolate *with* your mate, you may be able to get those good feelings going and rev up your romance, too! A recent study at Emory University found that if dopamine (key chemical released while eating chocolate) is injected into a female vole while she's in the presence of one particular male rodent, she later will pick out that rodent when he's in a crowd of other male rodents. She remembers the good chocolate lovin' feelings and wants that guy, and no other will do! (I hate the thought of animal testing, but at least in this case the little female rodent was made to feel very, very good.)

What if the female rodent had been injected with dopamine when *no* male rodents were present? It seems likely that when the herd came walking in, not only would she fail to seek out that any particular male—she'd probably ignore the whole lot of them! Who needs a man when you can get this good feeling all by yourself?

Unfortunately, this study, like most, leaves us with many more questions than answers. Would females of another species, like humans, respond the same way? How much chocolate would it take to produce that "dopey" dopamine effect that scientists were able to accomplish with a dopamine injection? Some scientists think it would take a ridiculous amount of chocolate to create a good dopamine high, but others disagree because of what we already know about our passion for chocolate.

That's why it's critical that *you* take this research to the next level. Do it for the sake of scientific advance. Do it for your *country!* Eat significant quantities of chocolate with your man present, preferably *naked!*

Now, we're smarter than rodents—arguably, anyway. You might ask, "Aren't we so smart that our consciousness and knowledge would get in the way and taint the results of research involving chocolate, our lover, and a private, comfy setting?" I have two answers to this:

1. Not necessarily. We may be talking about a brain chemistry connection that you have *no choice* but to make: eat chocolate + man present = man makes me feel good. Give me more of *that* man!

2. Who cares? This is a test involving chocolate and a man! Just do it!

72.

"Skin Heroin"

"We know too much and feel too little. At least we feel too little of those creative emotions from which a good life springs."
—Bertrand Russell

Oxytocin, one of the feel-good chemicals our bodies naturally produce and release, is sometimes referred to as "skin heroin." That's how powerful the effect can be.

Oxytocin is a natural chemical released in the brain and through the breast milk of a new mother whenever she's showing great love and care through nursing or cuddling. It's nature's way of rewarding a mother for being so patient with a little one and helping to ensure the baby's survival. Babies get it through the breast milk to calm them, too, also ensuring their survival by being sweet and docile if only for a few tender minutes.

What does this all have to do with romance? Everything. Nature does not just use oxytocin to induce good mothering. Oxytocin levels also increase during touching, cuddling, and other acts of foreplay, leading to a peak at orgasm. It's why women are much more receptive to sex if a fair amount of foreplay is included. During all that touching and tenderness, you're getting a brain chemical that helps you to relax and get in the mood!

A key message here is this: Don't ever feel like you're being too demanding or high-maintenance by wanting more foreplay, more cuddling. It's in your nature. Women who *don't* need more foreplay may be in the earlier stages of a romantic relationship (feel-good brain chemicals and hormones still running rampant) or possibly have a higher testosterone level (making them a little more man-like when it comes to sex drive). It's totally normal for a woman to need plenty of foreplay.

If getting in the mood, no matter how much foreplay, is nearly impossible for you, consider asking your doctor to test your hormonal levels, including testosterone. Get a new doctor if you don't feel that your concerns are being taken seriously.

Most of us have normal hormones and still just need a lot of foreplay to get in the mood. Nature created us the way we are for a reason. Not all of those reasons are fully understood by scientists or anyone else yet. But one thing we know is that in a normal relationship, the more you cuddle and participate in foreplay, the more passion there is in the relationship. If you've got a partner who doesn't understand your need for a lot of foreplay, he just needs to be reassured that your needs are perfectly normal and not a reflection on his manhood or sexiness.

Here's more good news about how oxytocin works and how we can use it to change the romance in our lives: oxytocin isn't just about sexual touching. It's believed to be triggered, to varying degrees, through all types of pleasant touching: hand holding, shoulder rubbing, hugs, playing footsie.

People who aren't the touchy-feely type need to break out of that shell and start touching their loved ones immediately. Scientists are linking lack of touch to everything from developmental disorders in babies to early senility in older people. The more you touch, the more you want to touch and be touched. You'll be healthier, happier, smarter, and more romantically inclined.

73

Strip Down to Your Freudian Slip

"We are never so defenseless against suffering as when we love."
—Sigmund Freud

If the same old arguments are standing in the way of romance and intimacy, it's time to take drastic measures. It's time to "go Freudian" on those old broken records.

Once you've been in a relationship with a person for a few years, it's typical to start assuming that you're now free of old, unwanted influences. Sure, your parents had a rotten marriage, but you're over that, right? Yes, he grew up in a loving, but very financially poor (or filthy rich) home—but that has nothing to do with *your* relationship, right?

The truth is, those early influences, good and bad, stay with us (and whatever relationships we have) forever.

We don't have to be "scarred" by an ugly past for our past to have a negative effect on our relationships. In some ways, I think it may even be harder for people who came from "perfect" homes and families to adapt to romantic relationships and families of their own. *My parents did it this way, so that's the best way. They obviously knew what they were doing. Any other way must be inferior!* How many good relationships must be at risk of being screwed up by these beliefs, carried by people from "perfect" family backgrounds?

To re-examine your past in a nonthreatening way, plan a dinner date with your lover. Ask him to jot down themes from recurring arguments you have: money, housekeeping contributions, child rearing, communication, whatever. Promise each other that you'll look at all these issues impersonally and without blame, without defensiveness, and without reliving the arguments all over again. Ask him if he'll help you examine how your respective upbringings *might, just might* have some kind of influence on the recurring arguments.

It was only after the honeymoon was over that my husband, Gary, and I became aware of our intense clash of cultures. It came as a shock. Both of us coming from loving families with parents who had been married forever, we assumed that it would all be a cinch. How could we fail, both of us having such great role models for marital success? It only took a few arguments for us to recognize that our families, while happy and seeming to have it all, were vastly different and those differences were steering us toward an all-out war.

Here's the gist of our dirty laundry: Gary's parents are the epitome of perfect politeness. If they have something unpleasant to say to one another, they find the right moment, in private, and then discuss calmly, rationally.

My parents, on the other hand, yelled. A lot.

At first, Gary, assuming that politeness was the *only* way, was beside himself to see how I would confront him at any moment over any little thing. He thought I was a barbarian. I was starting to think I had married Winston Churchill, and the stiff politeness and cold-shouldering was about to drive me nuts.

It was a real relief, in fact, when we discovered the root of our problem. Gary and I were either going to kill each other or set our own family style of communicating. We learned we would have to blaze our own trail, since his parents' way didn't work for me, and mine certainly didn't work for him.

Other culture clashes have come up over the years, and it's really difficult to realize what's going on beneath the surface before things start getting hostile. You have to distance yourself from the argument and recognize what's really going on.

If your partner has a tough time expressing feelings, don't be upset if you have to play the role of an interviewer. It's not *how* you get to the sharing that's important, just that you get there.

Sometimes digging into the past brings up memories that are more than you can handle alone. Counseling is worth the investment, and many employers offer a package of free counseling sessions through qualified organizations. Take advantage of it.

You only have a choice about your future together if you take the time to recognize how your separate pasts may be imprisoning you. Talking to each other, leaning on each other as you take inventory of the stuff from your past that you're still carrying around is a great way to forge a new, intimate bond.

74

Love and Laughter

"Laughter is the closest distance between two people."
—Victor Borge

t's my personal, scientifically unsubstantiated belief that laughter is a fantastic aphrodisiac. If your romance could use a boost, chances are your sense of humor could, too.

We need to invest more time in laughter. Here's why:

Laughter:
- Promotes creativity and makes problem solving easier.
- Encourages physical healing and overall good health. Your immune system is even known to get an extra boost when you laugh.
- Is an aerobic workout, using the diaphragm and stomach muscles.
- Tells other muscles not being used in the act of laughing to relax— making you feel more relaxed all over.
- Is a great cardiac workout and can aid in lowering blood pressure (for women more than men).
- Reduces neuroendocrine hormones associated with high stress.
- Triggers the release of endorphins.
- May help fight cancer.

If romance is what you need more of in your relationship and your life, more laughter will get you at least halfway there. If you need some inspiration, might I suggest a refresher course in literary classics? No, not Charlotte Brontë. Try Erma Bombeck. God rest her romance-starved soul; Erma wrote such classics in marital understanding as *A Marriage Made in Heaven or Too Tired for an Affair*, a book that still rings true with wives everywhere.

Every time I think I'm all alone in the world, one dirty sock away from strangling my husband, I turn to Erma, and five minutes later she has me in stitches. Married to a man she described as being terminally unromantic, Erma knew exactly how to draw humor from everyday situations in the life of an overworked wife and mother. She made women laugh and feel connected to one another as they all trudged on with pride in relationships, families, and *bodies* that could hardly be described as perfect. Women need more humor in their lives, and the world definitely needs another Erma Bombeck.

Lucille Ball is another woman who really understood women and relationships. Her wisdom and humor are timeless. She understood the dream and myth of a perfect marriage and home life and delighted in not living up to it. On a really down day, thirty minutes of *I Love Lucy* is guaranteed to bring you back into good cheer.

Another very funny loser at love is the comedic genius Merrill Markoe. She's written a number of funny books in the humor section and joyfully tells stories about her less-than-idyllic adventures in love. By the way, she's the writer/producer who made (ex-boyfriend) David Letterman a household name, another relationship that was hysterically far from perfect. Her book *How to Be Hap-Hap-Happy Like Me* had me laughing out loud.

I encourage you to find some female inspirations, too. Make it someone who can always make you laugh, whether it's an actress, writer, comedienne, or your wise next-door neighbor.

I'll mention one male inspiration for laughter, only because it's probably someone you've never heard of: Jim Mullen. If you haven't read his book *It Takes a Village Idiot*, don't walk, *run* to your nearest bookstore and buy it immediately. You'll laugh out loud as you read the story of his moving to the country with his wife.

I strongly recommend that you create a corner, somewhere in your world, where you keep things (books, movies, etc.) guaranteed to put you in stitches in a few minutes. A nightstand is a great place for that kind of stuff. So is an office at home, if you're lucky enough to have one. Wherever you find room, maintain your own little laughter collection. Review it often to remind you that it's there and waiting for those moments when you really need to lighten up.

Laughter helps us gain perspective on any problem. Referring to your humorous collection is also really helpful right in the middle of a fight that's getting out of control. I'm telling you, *I Love Lucy* can really save your marriage!

You may wonder what laughter has to do with romance. Answer: everything. Don't forget what I said about endorphins; plus, laughter relaxes you. Half the romance battle for women is getting relaxed. Laughter accomplishes this and more.

You might even get inspired to be funnier at home. Do funny things and make your mate/family laugh out loud. There's nothing more romantic than that! Humor is a powerful thing, and you don't have to be a comedic genius to use it to your advantage.

75

Make Love, Not Botox

"No spring, nor summer beauty hath such grace,
As I have seen in one autumnal face."
—John Donne

t's official: sex makes you look younger. It's yet another reason why we have to give romance a better chance in our lives, pulling out all the stops to encourage its flourishing.

Dr. David Weeks, a clinical neuropsychologist at Scotland's Royal Edinburgh hospital, studied 3500 people and found that sex actually slows the aging process. You can read his full findings in *Secrets of the Superyoung.*

One study found that people of the same age, standing side by side, were estimated to be different ages. The one who has more sex looks younger, the one who has less, older. And it's not just a two or three year difference perceived. People who have more sex are often guessed to be ten years younger than they really are.

When I first read this research, I have to admit I thought, sure, some sex-crazed forty-year-old woman is going to look younger than her relatively unsexed counterpart. If you're obsessed with sex, you're probably also dressing like a teenager, starving yourself to be thin, bleaching the living daylights out of your hair, and getting collagen injections to give your lips that pouty look.

But all the research I've read describes the sexed and unsexed guinea pigs of the study as otherwise "normal." It is, however, probably true that with frequent sex, you feel a little happier and more motivated to fix yourself up and dress in a way that's most becoming to your sexy self.

It's amazing how much money Americans spend annually in the pursuit of a youthful appearance. Our doctors tell us that there are things we can do naturally to look younger: exercise more, eat better, drink eight glasses of water every day. Finally, an answer that's fun and easy! Make love three times a week or more and they might not even recognize you at your next high school reunion. (*Who brought the teenager, and why is she hanging on Jan's husband?*) Well, we can fantasize.

76

The Romance of Contraception

*"The torment of precautions often
exceeds the dangers to be avoided."*
—Napoleon Bonaparte

*H*ow do you keep a romantic moment burning in passion, even as you deal with the decidedly *un*romantic chore of avoiding an unwanted pregnancy?

You've probably heard advice from sex therapists on how to make contraceptive devices a part of the erotic experience. I've read advice on how to turn the application of a condom into a full-fledged erotic gymnastics routine, choreographed to a Tina Turner song. But since sex and romance are not the same, the question remains: how do you make contraception *romantic*?

The answer is surprisingly simple. Just as you realize new ways to make every day of your life more romantic, likewise you can take every part of the sexual experience and make it more intentional and meaningful.

When you are about to use whatever contraceptive method you employ, make it a sexy moment—but also think about what it is that you're doing. The two of you are choosing to keep your life just as it is at this moment. If you're a newlywed, you may be saying *I want to live in this chapter of our marriage for a little while longer. I want to get to know every inch of you and grow as a couple before this family grows.* Now that's romantic! If you can just take a split second to think about the romantic choice you're making, you can take contraception from an annoying task to a romantic, meaningful moment.

The more mature couple, who may or may not have children, can use that same moment to say *I love my life with you right now. I cherish what we have and who we are as a couple right now.* Also a very romantic statement.

One word of caution about taking the pill to avoid the whole contraception issue—some studies suggest that chemical changes in a woman's body when she's on the pill may affect both partners' interest in sex.

Since the pill simulates pregnancy, pheromone changes and all, it may interfere with a woman's ability to feel arousal and with a man's ability to feel arousal for *her.* So if passion is what you're looking for, the pill may not be your best bet for contraception. All the more reason to find ways to keep the romance alive with other contraceptive methods.

Contraception, if you're creative, doesn't have to be a thirty-second time-out from a passionate moment. And it can even be romantic. Just take a moment to think about the choices you are making as a couple, and then celebrate that choice as part of the romantic experience.

77

Exercise Your Right to Romance

"If you would get exercise, go in search of the springs of life."
—Henry David Thoreau

I t never fails. Women who firm up and get rid of a few unwanted pounds feel sexier and more romantic. It's something we do for us, not our mates. Most men think we're beautiful exactly as we are, Rubenesque curves and all. And we should feel good about ourselves no matter what size or shape we come in. But it's an irrefutable fact that the closer we come to achieving our own personal best, the better, sexier, and more sensuous we feel about our own bodies.

Notice that I said *personal best*, as opposed to size-six jeans. As you work toward your own perfect body, feel great about it—whether your goal is reaching a size sixteen or a size four. Throw out all your magazines that subscribe to a one-size-fits-all feminine ideal. They're demeaning. They bring you down, and it's high time that women everywhere brought them down! Same goes for the misogynist fashion designers and personal trainers who think everyone with body fat over three percent is weak and lazy. But enough with my tirade over society's cruel and self-serving views that make the diet industry a multi-billion dollar venture in our country. Let's get back to focusing on us.

Exercise, even just for the sake of exercising (rather than weight loss) will make you feel better. There's more to it than just our psychological body issues. Exercising gives you more energy for anything you want to take on. Exercise will enable you to eat more and have more fun during romantic dates, eating what you want and enjoying yourself. You've already heard that exercise causes the release of endorphins, one of the feel-good brain chemicals also released during lovemaking.

Endorphins are released through aerobic exercise. The exercise has to be strenuous in order to get the endorphin release. Swimming, running, cycling, yoga, aerobics—all of them can potentially give you that coveted runner's high. The great news about endorphins is that you can feel that high for two to three hours during and following an intense workout.

But to get any of these benefits, you have to find an exercise plan that's right for you. And there's only one *right* plan: the kind you enjoy. You can have exercise experts talk to you until they're blue in the face about what constitutes a "good workout," but if it's not enjoyable to you, you won't stick with it, so it's worthless advice. Find something you enjoy and do it.

In fact, one of the best physical trainers I ever interviewed told me that her secret to success with clients was showing up at their house and, rather than worrying about a complicated formula (like ten minutes of warming up, ten minutes of stretching, twenty-five minutes of aerobic activity, ten minutes of cooling down, followed by seven minutes of stretching) she just asked them what they felt like doing on that day. Biking? Hiking? Running? Wanna run to the coffee shop, then walk back? Feel like skipping? Dancing? She made it fun every day by changing the scenery and leaving her clients' options open. Once they were really feeling and seeing some of the benefits of being active, she worked them into something tougher—or not. It all depended on where the client wanted to go with the workout, and this trainer was smart enough to know that the client was in charge and would quit exercising altogether if it wasn't fun anymore.

Even if you can't afford a trainer or don't want one, you can learn something from the best trainer I ever met. Do something physical every day that sounds appealing to you. If the only physical thing you enjoy doing is dancing, by God, go dancing! As long as it gets your heart pumping and your body sweating, that's good enough to get you started.

There have been some really interesting studies lately on losing weight and keeping weight off. I love studies that support the power of common sense. Studies show that diets don't work. People lose weight, but most gain it all back eventually, and many add to their weight. The people who keep it off combine sensible eating with exercise. One study found that the real secret may be in steps. People who successfully keep weight off take an average of four thousand steps a day. Nowhere does it say that the steps need to be incorporated into a workout routine, although to take four thousand steps (the equivalent of about four miles) requires a different level of effort for each person. If your job has you walking all the time, four thousand steps is easy. If you sit at a desk all day, it's going to require a lot more effort and time commitment.

Exercise is critical for the millions of women who let their poor body image keep them from enjoying sex. It ranks consistently among the top reasons why women say they're not comfortable with or interested in sex, even with spouses who adore them exactly the way they are. Tragic.

If you can get past the body-image glitch, the good news is that sex itself is fantastic exercise. Research shows that having sex three times a week for one year has the same health benefits as running seventy-five miles over the course of the year. Both activities burn about 7500 calories. If you wanted to make love *every day*, just imagine the health benefits! Plus, you don't have to exert yourself to the point of pain or physical exhaustion to get the runner's high that the rest of the population on the treadmill are killing themselves to reach.

The simple message is this: do something. Anything. Be creative about it and make sure you enjoy it. That's the only rule that counts. Love your body.

78

Catnap Before Romance

"Idleness, like kisses, to be sweet must be stolen."
—Jerome K. Jerome

t's the end of a very long day and you're exhausted. Sex is the last thing on your mind. Naturally, that's the moment when your mate feels his friskiest. All you want to do is climb into bed and get some rest, but you don't want to turn him away because you do care about him, his needs, and his feelings.

Good news! You don't have to choose between much-needed rest and romance. A significant nap, longer than one hour but less than two, will put you in prime form for a rendezvous.

Sex expert and columnist Rebecca Rosenblat ("Dr. Date") says it's advice she dishes out often.

"You should sleep for ninety minutes and *then* let him pursue sex," she says. "Studies show a woman's libido experiences a sudden surge after about ninety minutes of sleep."

I was floored when I first heard this information. This is the type of news-you-can-really-use that they should be plastering on billboards everywhere! But if it's news to you, it's most definitely news to *him,* and you'll have to find the right opportunity to share.

Tell your mate you stumbled across this fascinating fact at a moment when he is *not* already nibbling on your ear. In my experience, it makes for great Sunday brunch conversation. Then, the next time you walk in the door exhausted and come face to face with his obvious need for nookie, you can casually remind him of the information and suggest you take a little catnap.

Dr. Date advises that the man should be the one to take the initiative in a potential romantic moment temporarily delayed by extreme fatigue. "He should say, 'Listen, you rest. And in about an hour and a half, I'm going to give you a nice massage,'" suggests Rosenblat.

It creates a wonderful win-win situation. You get to bed early, get some rest, while he watches ESPN undisturbed (preferably *not* in the bedroom). And as icing on the cake, you both get great romance.

79

Hug Twelve Times a Day

"Devils can be driven out of the heart by the touch of a hand on a hand, or a mouth on a mouth."
—Tennessee Williams

It's become a common belief among "touch therapy" experts that we all need four hugs a day just for survival...eight hugs for maintenance...and twelve hugs daily for growth.

Most research on the benefits of hugs has been directed at drug-addicted and prematurely born babies, people who suffer from chronic pain, and orphans in war-torn countries. But in each of the cases, the findings were staggering. Hugs could do what drugs could not. Hugs could accomplish what years of other types of therapy had failed to accomplish. And while scientists are just starting to scratch the surface of the power of hugs for people with chronic and life-threatening conditions, who knows what kind of measurable effects the simple hug might have on us in terms of romantic relationships and family relationships?

One thing scientists *do* know is that hugs cause measurable physiological changes in the hugger and the huggee. Hugs also positively affect levels of cortisol, a hormone released to help us deal with severe stress.

Why are hugs so powerful? In a universal language, they tell us that we are loved, we are cared for. They tell us that we are worthy of love. Hugs tell us we are not alone in this world.

You can't give someone a real hug and harbor hostility toward them. It's virtually impossible. Some therapists swear that if you hug someone enough, you will feel the whole energy of a relationship change before your eyes. Some recommend twelve hugs a day for any relationship that needs mending or improving.

A friend told me once that when her children were upset, even as they entered the difficult teenage years, she would hug them, and as she did, she would actually feel their tension melt away.

I, like a lot of people, have never been a particularly "huggy" type of person. When I was a kid, all I wanted was a heartfelt hug that lasted maybe two seconds, then I was off to play. There *is* a certain amount of personal taste that accompanies the issue of hugging.

But when I became a parent, I instantly understood the value of touch. I wasn't just doing it for my baby girl; I got as much out of it as she did. I'm lucky that although she's not a baby anymore, she delights in cuddling.

Can a hug make a relationship more romantic? You bet it can. Hugging a spouse who is reluctant to talk about romance or any problem can eventually break down that wall of resistance. Hugging provides the relaxation and the touch that men and women need, and that women *especially* need in order to switch gears and start feeling romantic. A night of side-by-side hugging while sitting by a fire or watching shooting stars is the definition of a perfect, romantic date. And hugging is something romantic that can be done in public without embarrassment or timidness. Frequently hugging a partner tells him that his feelings are safe and he can open his heart without fear of rejection or abandonment. Nothing paves the way for great romance like creating a place where one feels safe.

Some people even think of hugs as "too romantic." While most schools encourage the slogan "hugs, not drugs," a school district in Minnesota unofficially banned hugging because school officials thought students were hugging each other too much and decided that hugs were "sexual and inappropriate." Students fought back, saying the forty to sixty hugs a day they received made them feel better and were a safe way of expressing their feelings. Many students there are willing to accept the consequences that come, whatever they may be, because they believe that the hugs they get are worth any price.

What if everyone got forty hugs a day? Can you imagine how it might transform the world? Most adults, according to surveys, say they get one or fewer hugs a day. Some say they can't remember the last time they got a hug.

It makes me think: if solving the world's problems starts in the home, why not start with a hug?

Hugs are romantic in a way that goes way beyond roses and moonlight. Hugs squeeze us right down to the soul level. They warm us to the bone. They give us hope and reassurance. Romance needs all those things to thrive.

A few more benefits of hugs include:

- Hugs may actually ward off illness.
- Hugs have been known to aid insomnia.
- They relieve chronic pain when nothing else, including drugs, works.
- They cure anxiety.
- They may be a fountain of youth! Hugs have been shown to keep people younger, physically and mentally.
- Hugs may fight or prevent dementia in seniors.
- They may be an effective diet aid. Hugs keep you from snacking too much.

The answer to your health and emotional problems could be in hugs. Twelve a day, to be exact.

"Words, like Nature, half reveal
And half conceal the Soul within."
—Alfred, Lord Tennyson

*L*et's face it. Cyber sex, if you've ever engaged in it, gets old real fast. It's like looking at pornographic pictures: shocking at first, then, mere moments later, painfully dull. Cyber sex is *not* romantic and is highly overrated. Cyber *romance* is where it's really at!

How can you be cyber romantic? Think Elizabeth Barrett Browning and Robert Browning. Can you imagine the kinds of emails that would have gone back and forth between the two of them if they had the benefit of instant messaging back then?

If you don't know what I'm talking about and can't imagine what really romantic correspondence is like, then check out the book *Sonnets from the Portuguese: Illuminated by the Brownings' Love Letters*. In it are the poems of Elizabeth intermingled with letters considered the most celebrated correspondence of the century and beyond.

Practice sending email to your lover that tells him that he is in your heart every second of every day. The Brownings were masters at expressing how the love for each other had a cataclysmic effect on their beings. I often wonder if their thinking about it so much and writing about it often gave the love even more power and meaning. It would have been impossible for the two to grow apart or let the romance drift away like you hear so many couples complain about. When you're writing about it *every day,* romance can't possibly elude you.

Use email to tell your lover why thoughts of them make you smile throughout your busy day. Tell him what it's like to know that you'll be coming home to them at the end of the day. Remind him of his qualities that, when reflected upon, feel like warm water running over your body. Tell him why he's different from anyone else you know. Tell him why he's special.

Set a cyber-scene for romance. Tell him you're looking forward to dinner by candlelight and invite him to a moonlit stroll tonight. Ask him if he'll sit in front of a crackling fire with you tonight while you give each other foot rubs and talk about all the things that are on the right track in your life together.

Tell him *why* you love him and no other. Tell him he's your hero and your warrior. Don't do it expecting that he's going to be able to respond just like Mr. Browning. Give cyber-love for the sake of giving and know that it will come back to you in whatever form he feels most comfortable with. If he responds to your loving cyber-words by doing something deeply romantic like taking your car out to have the oil changed, consider it an act of deep, passionate love from a guy who is very busy and still takes the time to make sure his darling doesn't break down on the highway somewhere. It *is* romantic if you allow it to be. If he *is* capable and comfortable with reciprocating sweet words of romance by email, so much the better! You'll quickly take your relationship to a new level of loving kindness and romance.

There's no question that email is one of the easiest ways to communicate these days. It's less jarring and usually better received than calling someone by landline or cell phone—much less paging someone. Nobody reads or answers their email unless they have a moment to do so. So take advantage of it by using it to build romance. You may find it easier to "say" things on a computer screen that you'd never say in person. That's the great thing about writing. You can erase, revise, spell-check, and write things you'd never have the guts to say aloud.

Everyone appreciates romantic email. Finding a nice note in between corporate memos and spam is the nicest, most romantic treat in a busy day!

81.
Be Afraid

*"There are times when fear is good. It must keep
its watchful place at the heart's controls."*
—Aeschylus

Who knew Alfred Hitchcock could be so sexy? Not the actual Hitchcock, but his movies really do have an effect that's a perfect primer for romance.

Medical researchers find very little difference between the physical reaction to fearful stimuli and sexual arousal. You can use this to your best romantic advantage by incorporating a touch of fear into your dates. That could simply mean going on a roller-coaster ride. It could mean taking in a suspenseful movie. Or you could even try more thrilling feats like taking hang-gliding lessons, or going white-water rafting, skydiving, or rock climbing.

Be sure to take full advantage of the moment and the physical response by planning some alone-time shortly after feeling the flood of fear. If you're seeing a movie, you may want to make it a drive-in. If you're going skydiving or rock climbing, have a hotel room ready for romance immediately following or find a private place.

Probably the easiest and most convenient way of feeling the thrill of fear and then capitalizing on it romantically is to just rent a great Hitchcock movie and park it on the couch together. And be sure to eat popcorn while you're at it. There's evidence that popcorn is a good brain food. It helps keep your mind alert, and great romance starts in the mind.

Once you've got the blood pumping and your heart thumping loudly, a great romantic moment becomes easy to surrender to.

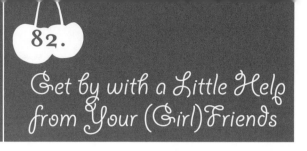

82

Get by with a Little Help from Your (Girl)Friends

"Intimacies between women often go backwards, beginning in revelations and ending up in small talk without loss of esteem."
—Elizabeth Bowen

Every now and then, my dad says something very wise. It's hard for me to believe that one of his wisest sayings came when he was so young, before I was born.

My mom and dad were barely out of the wedding chapel when my dad said, "Now let's get something straight right now. I cannot be your sole source of entertainment. If this is going to work, you're going to have to have your own thing and your own friendships to help make your life happy and fulfilling."

Even at twenty-three years old, my dad understood that a man can't fulfill all of a woman's needs, even, and especially, her needs for intimacy.

Much of our need for intimacy and even romance is fulfilled through meaningful friendships with other women. When we don't cultivate and nurture those friendships or don't lean on them like we should, the result can be too much pressure placed on our soul-mate relationship. He can't be your *everything,* no matter what the ballads and poets say.

Much has been said lately about the benefits of female friendship, most prominently that we're awash with the feel-good brain chemical oxytocin when we indulge in a gabfest with a close girlfriend. Talking with a female confidante doesn't just make us feel better, it makes us healthier and more balanced.

Girlfriends fill a need for intimacy that men cannot and should not be asked to fill. When we talk with our girlfriends and feel that loving connection, when we give each other a hug and cry over each other's problems, when we search for solutions and find a helping hand, our mate's intimacy "to do" list becomes that much shorter and less urgent.

With girlfriends handy, your mate is not required to be your best friend, confidant, *and* Romeo. He's free to be your lover, partner, and friend. It's the way it should be.

83.
Save the Whales

"To serve is beautiful, but only if it is done with joy and a whole heart and a free mind."
—Pearl S. Buck

When the honeymoon is officially over, it's the perfect time to recapture romance by working for common causes and toward common goals.

Just look at some of the most successful, lasting, and admirable relationships around and tell me that working toward a common cause doesn't work wonders. Think of Jimmy Carter and his wife, Rosalynn. When Jimmy isn't off accepting the Nobel Peace Prize for helping to find diplomatic solutions to world conflicts, he and his wife are building houses for Habitat for Humanity. They swear that it's given them more than they have given of themselves.

Some relationship experts and researchers believe that while couples can't turn back the clock to return to the pheromonally-crazed early days of a relationship, they may actually be able to achieve greater heights in romantic and sexual chemistry by working together on mutual interests and common missions.

For you, just like the Carters, that could mean finding a charitable cause you're both passionate about. It could mean volunteering for a political campaign you both support. Working together at the church might be the ticket.

The key is finding something you're *both* enthusiastic about. It can't be something that has passionate support from one of you and only lukewarm interest from the other.

Make a list of possible projects and rate them on a scale of one to ten, ten being something that you could devote lots of time to and of which you'd never get tired. Of course, most of us have only a certain amount of time to give, so commit to a certain number of hours every month that you'll spend together, working toward a common cause.

If you have kids, you may want to include them in the fun. Teach them while they're young about the joys of giving back to the community and working to help make the world a better place.

The possibilities for a common, rewarding cause are limitless. We've all seen couples who seem so happy together, so much like an unstoppable team. Maybe we've see them at church or working in the neighborhood and wondered what their secret was. The secret is right before our eyes: working together on something that makes the world a better place. Think of it as passion in action.

"We should consider every day lost on which we have not danced at least once."
—Friedrich Nietzsche

When was the last time you and your sweetheart danced for joy? Not the waltz, not the Texas two-step, not the rock'n'roll moves that you take while calculating the "coolness" of every subtle gyration and swivel. I mean dancing with wild abandon.

Can you remember the last time you danced together like there was nobody looking and you couldn't care less whether you looked ridiculous doing it? For most of us, such memories are so far in the distant past, or so foggy from too much wine at a company Christmas party, that we can't possibly recall the wonderful effects of dancing for sheer joy.

Even in the beginning of our relationship, Gary and I did not really dance together like that. Oh, sure, we'd do the obligatory slow dance, or halfhearted (don't want to be a party pooper) bounce for three minutes, until we could make our escape.

Like lots of other couples, our usual mode was to sit at our table smiling and watching in disbelief as a few couples made complete idiots of themselves on the dance floor. We thought we were so smart and too cool to avoid that embarrassing trap—we couldn't have been more wrong. Those couples out there on the dance floor, with their two left feet and enormous wiggling rear ends, were getting high doses of endorphins and double shots of romantic feelings.

These days, my husband and I like to dance and sing to the Rolling Stones. We've always loved the Rolling Stones but used to just sway and bob, ever so slightly, to their music. Now we wrack our old bodies in all directions to the beat, adding air guitars and air drums wherever possible. Sometimes we honor our friends and strangers with this special visual feast, but it's usually just us.

Dancing for joy has truly added new dimensions to our romance. Music has power that predates history. Dancing to the beat (or even *off* the beat if you have no sense of rhythm, like me) has immense magic. Just letting go and experiencing it, in whatever way feels right to you, breathes new life into your romantic, sexy nature. It's primal and powerful, but *only* if you really let go, really stop caring what you look like, and dance for pure joy!

section five

offbeat romance

85.

Rent a Single-Wide Trailer

"A man knows his companion in a long journey and a little inn."
—Thomas Fuller

Get away from it all by taking a romantic weekend for two in a tiny trailer in the middle of nowhere with terrible television reception, inclement weather, abysmal sightseeing, and otherwise very, very little to do in the way of entertainment. Go somewhere where the townspeople will be shocked to see tourists. Go someplace you've never gone and never wanted to!

This romantic idea is perfect for the couple who has seen the world, but failed to see *each other* lately. Have you ever been in a trailer in the woods that gets almost no television or radio reception? I have. I know it sounds peaceful, and it is. For about five minutes. Then you either start desperately messing with the television's rabbit ears, or you get very creative about ways to pass the time.

Sure, you can *try* to take in the tourist experience...go to town, eat in the only diner, shop in the one store, visit the only monument. But how long can you possibly drag on this kind of excitement? Not long. Before you know it, you're back in the single-wide, lookin' for love.

Who knew a town like the one I'm describing could turn into the romance capital of the world? All the residents, that's who. You'll notice during your visit to the only store in town that it carries an amazing selection of baby supplies.

Visiting a town like this (I won't ruin the serenity of the town we visit by revealing its name) can bring you and your lover together like never before. You're all you've got for entertainment. All you need is a clean room and a dirty novel to read aloud, and you're in business.

Outdoorsy friends of mine promise that you can achieve the same kind of closeness while backpacking. Says one friend, "Once you get there and set up the tent, there's really not much else to do!"

86.

Nurture Your Inner Slut

"Women are like tricks by sleight of hand,
Which to admire, we should not understand."
—William Congreve

I honestly don't know why this is, but many of my friends and friendly acquaintances who used to be on the slutty side in their younger years are now completely normal—that is to say, practically asexual. And interestingly, those who used to be "prudes" are now of questionable virtue.

Perhaps the sexually overt women managed to get all those wild, carnal cravings out of their systems. And perhaps all the prudes came to realize that there is no pot of gold or giant prize waiting for them after years spent being sexually repressed and forever the good girl.

I only had one friend who seemed to have it together, sexually speaking, in our younger years. She looked out for herself, made her own choices based on what she wanted and not what anyone else did, and was always happy. She never slept with anyone in a hopeless attempt to make him love her. She never abstained from sex in an effort to maintain some ridiculous image of feminine perfection, good and wholesome in every way, exactly the kind of girl *his mother* dreams about and prays he'll marry.

She didn't care about getting married, though if she met the right guy, she had no aversion to the idea. She had somehow escaped all the female games and roles society teaches us to play. She took care of her own sexual needs and was sensitive to others' needs, but not overly so.

I remember that back then I incorrectly placed her in the "slut" category and now realize that I couldn't have been more wrong.

I now envy the healthy attitude she had all along toward female sexuality. And, while I have no regrets about learning what I learned throughout my single years in Prudesville, I have finally found myself willing to nurture my inner slut.

If you happen to be married, as I am, nurturing your inner slut is easier in some ways, harder in others.

For example, if you're single and you suddenly start taking care of your sexual needs (keeping safety always in mind, of course) without worrying constantly about whether you're giving the milk away for free, or whether he'll keep calling you or want to marry you or whatever...no man in your life is going to start quizzing you relentlessly, demanding to know what's with the change in you. (Although the answer should be easy: "I'm nurturing my inner slut! That's the change.")

If you're married and you suddenly start attacking your husband as he walks in the door because you realize that your inner slut needs to be expressed that day—and you physically use him up and then toss him aside when you're finished with him like an empty pint of Ben & Jerry's, he *will* ask questions.

But I think you'll find that most husbands are completely cool with the idea of being your sexual plaything—to be used up and manhandled in any old way. They may ask questions, but not many. Ultimately, they won't care and will be very, very pleased by the demon possession, amnesia attack, or whatever it is that suddenly changed you. They truly don't care, as long as it means good sex.

How can you nurture your inner slut? Think of yourself for a change. Ask yourself, "*What could I do today to sexually fulfill ME?*" Ask, "*What would be the best way for me to 'get some' TODAY?*" And then you'll come up with all kinds of appealing possibilities.

I'm not really talking about an outward transformation. I'm not suggesting that you start wearing a trench coat and sunglasses to the supermarket so you can flash the stock boy for kicks (but that *is* a thought); I'm only suggesting that you nurture your *inner* slut, the raw sexual side of you that occasionally would like to come out and play, even if she's only allowed to play late at night in the privacy of your own boudoir.

Your inner slut will not remain quiet forever. You can't keep her caged up and silenced eternally, or eventually she will break free with a roar and possibly some embarrassment.

A friend of mine, who shall remain nameless, used to be *way* on the prude side, like the grand empress of prudery and respectability. You just knew it couldn't last forever. One night she came into town, boyfriend on her arm, and wanted to spend the night in our guest room.

About a half hour after retiring for the night, my husband and I hear these unbelievably loud screams and wails. I didn't know moaning at that volume was even possible! There was so much banging and screaming, I couldn't decide whether to call 911 or my carpenter! Surely, there was going to be massive sheet-rock damage once this carnal craze finally ended! And—let me be clear—our guest room was one floor and fifteen hundred feet away from our master bedroom! This was some LOUD sex!

At long last, there was silence. But then minutes later it started all over again! I'm not talking about the kind of screaming and sexual-mauling hysterics that you can at least feel assured is only waking the dead within your *own home!* No, I was absolutely positive that it was loud enough for neighbors a block away to hear. (And we lived near the lake, so picture many, many houses crammed very close together with windows and sliding doors always open!)

The next day, my friend and her exhausted boyfriend left very early. Later in the day, neighbors who never knew we had company seemed to be overly smiley when they said, "Hi there" over the fence. Neighbors I hadn't seen in months made a special point of being very chatty. Some of them probably just wanted to ease their minds that what they heard was really just sexual fun and that I wasn't really bludgeoned to death, as they must have half feared.

My only point in telling you this very embarrassing story is that I'm thrilled that my friend finally got in touch with her inner slut. But I think it may have been so overdue that when she finally *did* welcome it, it rushed in like a crazed porn-star wannabe. Yikes!

I think what happened to my friend is a perfect example of the consequences of ignoring your inner slut for too long. She will not be denied, and when she finally makes her appearance by force, she comes out with a roar!

But, I should mention, my friend did seem pretty happy when she left my home that morning.

87

Make Every Date Unusual

> *"No pleasure endures unseasoned by variety."*
> —Publilius Syrus

I beg you to do one strange thing every single time you go out on a date with your sweetheart. Before you freak out, thinking I must be talking hard-core, realize this: you live in a bubble.

Most of us live lives of such routine and order, eating at a different restaurant might sound wildly exotic. I'm talking about doing one little, tiny (or big) different thing on every single date.

Routine is comfortable, familiar, and even cozy, and if you like, you can keep the *main course* in your happy little routine. All I'm suggesting is that you change the side dishes.

If he usually drives, *you* get behind the wheel one night. If you usually go to dinner and a movie, go to dinner and then roller-skating one night. Have him order your meal and vice versa—and commit to actually eating whatever you order for each other.

Why is doing something different on every date so important? Because it awakens the senses, and great romance begins in an alert and imaginative mind.

You should know that I love the familiar groove of a rut as much as anyone. I'll order the same dish every single time I go to one of our regular haunts. I'll order the same drink. I'll even try to get the same table.

The fantastic thing is that you only have to change one tiny element (the temperature of the room, the addition of candles) and the spell is broken. Order the same food, but take it out on the patio. Voila!

As we all know, routines don't just keep us ordering the same old things at restaurants or driving the same way home every single night, they also have a huge impact on romance. If you cling to routines in *one* area of your life, it's a sure bet that you gravitate toward them in *other* areas. Routines are mind numbing and romance deadening. And when it's dead, we forget what we have. We can't even *see* the possibilities for excitement and passion and new life that are all around us. Consider the possibilities!

The hardest part about breaking yourself free from the trance-like state that goes hand-in-hand with routine is thinking of new things to do. Creativity and *trance* are so very rarely partners in crime. So here are a few ideas for little, different things to do on dates—just to get the ball rolling:

- Bring a camera and ask someone to take pictures of the two of you. Make up an occasion, if someone asks. Maybe they'll send champagne to your table!
- Bring a book of poetry along, and while waiting for your food or standing in line for movie tickets, read a poem aloud. Actually, any book that moves you would do. For me it would be something from *Walden*. Or anything from Emerson.
- Try five minutes of French kissing at the *start* of your date.
- After dinner, go to the nearest body of water. Take your shoes off and wade. Get at least your toes wet.
- Go vegetarian for a night.
- Experience improvisational-style theater.
- Wear an outfit *he* bought you. One you've been avoiding.
- Go to a restaurant on karaoke night, and just do it! One song. It won't kill you.
- See an independent film.
- If you normally have alcoholic beverages with dinner, skip it for a night.
- Whatever your rule normally is regarding dessert, change it.
- Play footsie under the table.

- Find out where the older people in your town go to dance and then join them—you don't have to stay all night.
- Support the special events planned at a neighborhood church, even if it's not your religion. You'll probably get the cheapest night of food and entertainment around.
- Go bowling. (If this is part of your usual routine, change this one to "Go to a poetry reading.")
- Go fly a kite.
- See a fortune teller together, just for fun.
- Bring a book on palmistry on your date and try to interpret his palm. Have him do the same for you.
- Instead of going to the big-name musical in town, go to the tiny theater that's around the corner and down the street from the big theater.
- Wear really comfortable shoes and encourage your lover to do the same.
- Ask your kids, or the kids of a couple you know, to plan your date for you.
- Order the food a nearby table is enjoying, without even looking.

88.

Brigadoon

*"The wind in the grain is the caress to the spouse,
it is the hand of peace stroking her hair."*
—Antoine de Saint-Exupèry

They say that a true Scotsman wears nothing under his kilt. Not being a huge fan of the scratchy lace underwear that polls reveal men love so much, I think perhaps we women should take the advice of the Scotsman. On a date, wear your kilt and a smile. Let your lover know your secret.

I'm shocked rather easily, and it amazes me how many people reveal to me that underwear is something they regularly do without. "Freeing," they tell me, "Liberating, rejuvenating, *sexy!*" Call me a prude, but I'm still working up the nerve. But there's no reason why *you* shouldn't join the (apparent) masses of people who believe that less is definitely more.

If you live in the windy city of Chicago, this advice might be a little more dangerous. In my hometown of Seattle, the only danger is that your wool kilt will shrink in a heavy downpour. That could be dangerous, too.

Still, it may be worth the risk for the sake of romance. He will love it, even if you're fibbing and you're actually wearing enormous granny-style girdle underwear that cover everything and then some. He'll love just thinking that you might be *au naturel.*

Or you could try what a friend confides that she's done.

"Sashay off to the ladies room and come back with your little scrap of silk knickers in your hand. Reach down and give him a kiss, slide your arms down and put your panties in his pocket or on his lap. Whisper, 'I've got something for you.' Then sit down and act innocent and decorous for the rest of the meal."

"To be able to enjoy one's past life is to live twice."
—Marcus Valerius Martialis

*M*any romance "coaches" (yes, there are such services available) advise couples to relive a first date in order to rekindle romance. But few, if any, of them offer this priceless advice: dress and accessorize exactly as you would have in that era. You might have to raid a thrift store to achieve the look.

Imagine how much fun you'll have walking out the door in Madonna-style leggings with bobby socks and stiletto heels, a torn sweatshirt à la *Flashdance,* and hair sprayed up and out toward the ceiling like you've just gotten a dose of moderate electric shock. Gigantic earrings are a must, as are the fingerless lace gloves.

He'll be enchanted, your dashing date, as he greets you with his bi-level/mullet-style hairdo (You know what they say: *business in front, party in the back*). You'll think, *Thank God he wore a tie,* even if it is just a skinny, piano-key tie with a sleeveless T-shirt and a pastel-colored Miami Vice jacket. And his multicolored parachute pants will pull it all together.

If you find yourself thousands of miles away from the actual location of your first date, no worries. I'm sure you can find a TGIFridays in your new town, too.

And while you think you might have a tough time finding a place to go dancing to retro tunes, you're probably wrong. In Seattle, there's a club that plays '70s and '80s stuff exclusively and it's fantastically popular. If your town doesn't have a retro club, why not invite a few couples to dress up too and have a little "first date" party? It would make a sensational anniversary party theme.

The point of all this? Just have fun. For one night remember the simpler times...when all you needed was a Thompson Twins song, a Bartles & James wine cooler, a pair of leg warmers, a perm, and the one that you love.

Tattoo His Name On Your Ass

*"What is life but a series of inspired follies?
The difficulty is to find them to do."*
—George Bernard Shaw

A temporary tattoo, of course (you *really* don't want to have to explain it to your granddaughter someday in the swimming pool locker room).

But just imagine his shock and delight some night when you blind him with a full moon and tattoo of his name. You don't have to tell him it's a temporary. Let him think you've temporarily lost your mind. Let him think you're so nuts about him, you were just overcome with the idea of letting the whole world (or at least all the interesting folks at Steve's Tattoo and Body Piercing Emporium) know about your perfect, passionate love.

It's important that you *not* end the date with a steamy shower or with anything that involves massage oil. Keep the illusion going as long as you can.

If you are too embarrassed to take your *business* to the Tattoo Emporium, there are also a lot of companies on the Internet that offer custom tattoos or tattoo paper that will enable you to fashion your own body art with your computer and printer. Custom temporary tattoos that you can buy over the Internet are often sold in groups of a thousand (apparently, selling temporary tattoos is a big money-maker for cheerleading squads and sports teams). I saw a deal online for a thousand custom tattoos for $70. Just think, even with regular showering, you could deceive your mate for three years or more.

A heck of a deal!

91.

Ditch the Family for the Holidays

"The man does better who runs from disaster than he who is caught by it."
—Homer

If your family is like mine, the holidays are a time for the out-of-towners to crowd into your guest rooms and snuggle in just like they never moved away. I love having the family all together, but I also get really stressed out. In my family, *mi casa es su casa* is not just a nice phrase, it's cardinal law. Suggesting that someone in my family check into a hotel room is interpreted as a clear signal that you don't want them to come home for Christmas, that you'd rather they stay away from the family altogether, and you don't care if you never see them again. My family is a little melodramatic, maybe yours is too. But for some reason, hotels have always been seen as cold, impersonal, and totally out of the question.

While it's completely unforgivable to ask someone else in the family to stay at a hotel room, it's somehow considered almost acceptable and seemingly selfless if you graciously offer to give up your home for the weekend and check into a hotel *yourself.* Leave the kids and a stocked refrigerator with the relatives and go to a really nice hotel. Why didn't I think of this years ago?

Who would have thought that during the stress of the holidays you could find the time and energy to make mad, passionate love in a hotel room, knowing the kids are safe and sound, snuggling with aunts and uncles around the Christmas tree in *your living room?*

It may give you a whole new excitement for the holidays. My simple message is this: Even during the most stressful time of the year, you *can* find ways to keep the romance alive. Can you do this and still maintain the myth that for two weeks out of the year you are Mrs. Claus, the Sugarplum Fairy, and Martha Stewart all rolled into one nauseating holiday caricature? Probably not. But most of us were never really very good at the ultimate hostess sham anyway, so giving it up is really a gift to all concerned.

Turning your house over to the relatives gives someone else the chance to exhaust themselves by masquerading as the spirit of Christmas (or Hanukkah) incarnate. They'll enjoy the rare opportunity to be Queen Christmas, and you'll enjoy the plush bathrobe you get to borrow while staying in a nice hotel room for a few days. Imagine it: taking baths, ordering movies that you would never get to watch at home, room service with a rose. A morning newspaper at your doorstep that doesn't get dissected into nineteen different pieces before you get a chance to read it. Need I go on?

The holidays are typically a time of year when women overgive to everyone but themselves and their mates. Knock it off. You don't have to choose between Christmas morning with your children and a peaceful night's rest on Christmas. Your children will *not* be scarred for life if you spend a few nights around the holidays at the Holiday Inn. By taking care of yourself and enjoying a little secret romance, you might even help your children have more pleasant memories of Christmas. Think about it: Mommy drinking wine and exploding at Grandma for being critical about the dryness of the stuffing, *or* Mommy and Daddy happy, opening presents and hugging each other more than usual, Grandma still muttering critically about the dryness of the stuffing.

You might never succeed at turning the holidays into a haven of romance and carefree living, but why not give it a try? Give up your home and ditch the family.

92.
A Date at the Cemetery

"The fall of a leaf is a whisper to the living."
—English proverb

A romantic stroll, just the two of you, amid beautiful landscaping...in the cemetery.

It's probably the last place on Earth you'd think of having a date, and that's exactly why I'm suggesting it. That and the fact that cemeteries are almost always beautifully landscaped, with some of the best territorial views you can usually find—and they're almost always completely void of live people. Talk about privacy, seclusion, and potential for romance!

I know it seems odd, but the reason cemeteries are secluded is exactly why you should consider a romantic date there. Most people avoid cemeteries because they don't want to think about the reality: we're all going to die, sooner or later.

Where's the romance in this fact? The romance is in facing the truth and experiencing a revelation on how you choose to live.

If you constantly hide from the fact that your days are few in this life, you may never make serious choices about how you're spending your time and whether you're loving as much as you can love.

If you believe that you have all the time in the world, you can work fifteen-hour days without seeing your loved ones and think nothing of it. When you hide from the truth, you believe there's always another day to devote to someone you love.

Living a lie, you can tell yourself that it's really important to push yourself harder to acquire more material wealth and higher status in the company or the world.

The reason it's particularly easy for me to think of a cemetery as a romantic place to take a stroll with my husband is that there are some really beautiful ones in my neighborhood. I can never resist reading the headstones as I take in the views, the landscaping, and the total privacy. As I read the words on the marble, I'm powerfully touched by the things that people have inscribed for eternity. *Loving Wife, Mother, and Best Friend. We Love You Forever.*

Words like that are wonderful reminders to me of what I really want to be in this life, and how little time I might have to be just that.

We stroll, my husband and I, hand in hand through the perfectly manicured lawns and exquisitely landscaped gardens and experience the peace that comes with knowing what is really, really important.

Cemeteries remind me that in the end, all we really have is love, family, friendship. Love is the one and only thing that lives on and on and on. It's what we're here for. But it's not even enough to say, "I love you" every day. I have to show it.

You may still be unconvinced that cemeteries are romantic. But if you or your lover have been struggling to prioritize all the "important" things in your life, a peaceful stroll through the cemetery is an important lesson: Love fully for as long as you live.

93

Greet Him Like a Dog

*"The great pleasure of a dog is that you may make a
fool of yourself with him and not only will he not
scold you, but he will make a fool of himself too."*
—Samuel Butler

Dogs greet each other by checking out one another's rear ends. That's certainly not what I'm suggesting you do (unless it's a very special occasion). No, I'm referring to another little canine habit that's less likely to draw negative attention and stares. Meet him at the door when he comes home, and encourage him to do the same for you.

My dad had a little ritual with the beloved family dog, Katie, for years and years. Dad would come home, and in the foyer of our home he would vigorously pet Katie, scratch her belly, stroke her ears, talk lovingly to her. She lived for the attention from him and it made my mom pretty jealous.

"Why don't you ever lavish that kind of attention on *me?*" she would often complain.

"Because you don't come racing to the door when you hear me come in. You don't wag your tail to tell me how happy you are to see me. You don't give me a big, wet kiss. Katie is happy to see me, it's not like *any-body else is!*"

He had a point. None of the rest of us even bothered looking up from our books or away from the television when he walked in the door. We were just as inattentive to the arrival of any *other* member of the family, but that was beside Dad's point.

Katie was the only one in the family who made a romantic ritual of the comings and goings of the household. She displayed signs of genuine sadness to see us leave, and you could tell she'd be counting the hours until our return. Every time one of us walked through the door, it was as if we were coming home from the war. Kisses. Exuberance. Pure unabashed delight!

There was a time when we *all* greeted Dad or Mom at the door. But we had grown up and those days were over, and my Dad was just grateful to see that *somebody* cared.

How loving and romantic it is to greet someone at the door, the way you would a welcome guest. If you want a home filled with warmth and love, what greater place to start than by taking the time to greet each person warmly who enters? Many couples kiss good-bye and kiss hello, but how many actually *come to the door* for a greeting?

Can you imagine how it could change your entire night, maybe even your week, to have your sweetheart walk to the door, take your bags, give you a kiss, and tell you how happy he is to see you? Just the thought of it might make you feel so good that you won't wait for *him* to do it for you, perhaps you will take the first step and extend a display of love and affection that is so rarely seen these days. Just thinking about how happy you'll make him by meeting him at the door will cause your anticipation and excitement to build for his arrival.

As Katie got older, her greetings slipped a little. You could occasionally find her forgetfully snoozing through our arrivals, but never Dad's. Katie heard his car and would wait faithfully by the door...gray, hearing and sight impaired (Katie, not Dad), but still as excited as ever to see Dad come home. I'm convinced that it wasn't just Katie paying homage to Dad's "alpha dog" status. No, it was because Dad understood the other half of a warm welcome. He rewarded her bountifully every time she came to the door to greet him.

Katie and Dad can teach us another lesson here, too. When somebody bothers to get up and greet you at the door, take a moment to kiss them, hug them, and show them how much that means to you. You can tell them about your awful day later. The couch or refrigerator will wait another two minutes. Take a moment to accept a warm greeting and reconnect by hugging, kissing, and cuddling. Say, "Thank you so much" to the person who greets you, and then return the favor with a warm greeting at the door the next time they come home.

I believe that showing the effort of getting up and meeting someone for a greeting can change the whole energy in a relationship, and a home. Try it, you'll see. If you really want to make each other happy, greet each other like dogs!

94

Tempt Him with Flank

"Cooking is like love. It should be entered into with abandon or not at all."
—Harriet Van Horne

Cooked foods, all by themselves, have aphrodisiac qualities. When someone cooks for us, we feel nurtured and loved, and from there it's not a distant journey to romance. But there really *are* foods you can prepare on a special night that will increase the likelihood of your successfully steaming up more than just the kitchen.

Ruth Winter is the coauthor of *Smart Food* and *Brain Workout*. She's made it her mission to discover which foods, prepared in certain ways, can help us maximize the potential of our bodies and brains.

She graciously offered this book her suggestions on an entire menu aimed at keeping romance fresh on the mind and feasible for the body:

You might want to start with oysters, which have zinc. Zinc has been found to be good for male performance. The old saying about oysters being sexy really has some merit.

For the main dish, a flank steak or another type of steak with the fat removed may be intriguing because neurotransmitters are made from proteins and they will help keep you both awake. Besides, culture has a lot to do with romance, and most men think steak is a "man's meal."

For side dishes, Winter recommends vegetables like spinach or broccoli as long as they're not overcooked.

Pasta or fresh bread is especially helpful in keeping arguments at bay. Winter says carbohydrates keep things calm.

For beverages, a little alcohol (emphasis on the word *little)* can be just the thing to get the mind and body ripe for romantic thoughts.

Winter says, "A glass of wine, unless the lover has migraine headaches, would be relaxing. If alcohol is out, then tomato juice with a little lemon is a nice touch. It contains potassium, which is vital to the transmission of messages between your nerves."

For something different for dessert, try a banana soufflé. According to Winter, "Bananas have serotonin, a brain chemical which helps to keep you happy."

Don't forget candlelight, soft music, and a clean dining space to clear your mind of your worries and daily hassles. But the most important ingredient of all, concedes Winter, is attitude. "Above all, don't bring your troubles to the table." If you do, all the oysters in the ocean won't help in setting the stage for love.

It's worth mentioning at this point that I offer ideas on cooking, decorating, and all things domestic cautiously. I'd hate for anyone to think I'm telling women that to get romance, do the traditional, womanly thing in the home.

If you enjoy cooking, fabulous. If not, forget it (or try gourmet takeout). There are plenty of ways to attain the romance you desire. Make romance sing in your life—*your way.*

95

Don't Worry, Be Happy

"There is in every true woman's heart a spark of heavenly fire, which lies dormant in the broad daylight of prosperity, but which kindles up and beams and blazes in the dark hour of adversity."
—Washington Irving

No matter what poll or research you examine, women cite the same reason over and over again when asked why their interest in romance and romantic interludes is waning: we're stressed out.

Women walk a tightrope these days while juggling at least nine bowling pins. How can we be expected to drop the pins at a moment's notice and relax—just because the clock says "time for romance"?

We've got to unwind. We've got to learn to relax long enough to enjoy life for a few sweet hours. But how?

Well, the ultimate solutions are complicated and probably require the help of a therapist, a life-management coach, a personal assistant, a mind-reading housekeeper, a chef who can create brilliant meals with the only two clean pans available, and a live-in computer technician. Thankfully, there are simpler solutions that won't break the bank.

One thing you can do is force yourself to smile. This is a trick I learned when I was a fairly young, nervous news anchor. Even when you're seriously stressed out, a nervous wreck, or whatever ails you, if you can force yourself to find something to smile about and give the world a wide, toothy grin, you can fool your brain into thinking that everything is great. Your brain will release feel-good hormones and your muscles will cease clenching. You will relax. One important note though—it has to be a real smile. That's the tricky part. It can't be a fake smile. It has to do with the muscles around your eyes. With a phony smile, those muscles don't move, and the hormones don't get triggered. A real smile uses up your whole face, including the muscles around your eyes. Somehow, the "whole-face smile" triggers the release of the happy hormones.

And here's another temporary solution that's very simple: sing the international anthem of multitasking women everywhere: "Don't Worry, Be Happy" by Bobby McFerrin.

I have friends who hate this song, and who swear to me that I need to find a better example, like Bob Marley's "Three Little Birds." My husband insists Santana's "Simba Pa Ti" can make you feel the ocean's warm breeze and total serenity. Find whatever works for you, but I really think McFerrin's song is as potent as a double martini at the end of a very bad day.

Whenever I play this song in my car, it's like getting a massage and a life-saving transfusion all at the same time. It's amazing how a song can really ease your troubles and lower your blood pressure. Pretty soon, I'm not taking my dirty house so seriously, I realize the piled-up bills will get paid and then just pile up again, and I'm OK with it. This one silly song has the power to relax me and get me more in the mood for the romance that makes life worth living.

The song apparently had the same effect on billions of other people, because in the year that the song was named Song of the Year at the Grammys, it also hit the number-one spot on the charts in almost every country in the world!

It's an even more amazing song when you consider McFerrin created it on the spot, unrehearsed, totally impromptu in the recording studio.

But perhaps it's not that amazing when you consider where Bobby McFerrin's heart is. This a man who can teach all of us something about romance and love, because in spite of all his great success, awards, and international acclaim, he states that his greatest ambition is to spend as much time as possible with his wife and their three children. Our hero.

I highly recommend that you use "Don't Worry, Be Happy" or some other tranquilizing song to help you regularly find a place of peace in your life amid the chaos. While you're at it, try my "whole face" smiling technique. You'll be happier and you'll feel much more romantic, if only for a few hours every week. Then, you can get right back to juggling all those bowling pins on a tightrope.

You can buy "Don't Worry, Be Happy" directly from McFerrin's website at www.bobbymcferrin.com.

96

Utilitarian Romance

"Every day cannot be a feast of lanterns."
—Chinese proverb

It's hard for me to look at changing the oil in my car as deeply romantic. But it's yet another way we have to distinguish the differences between men and women and how each sex looks at being loving.

Many men have a hard time seeing the real value, the real contribution, in spraying the sheets with lavender water. It's almost impossible for many of them to accept that we could be really moved by such a worthless act.

But changing out your bald tires for a new set of all-weather radials—now *that's* an act of love!

I know it sounds like I'm being sexist. There are many men who understand and appreciate that it's the little things that drive a woman wild. But I'd like to make a simple argument in favor of the guy who *does* think that fixing a leaky faucet is the epitome of romantic.

If you're willing to look past his hind end sticking out from under the sink for hours and hours, you'll see a guy who is, in his own way, nesting. Just as we sprinkle lavender water on the sheets or buy fresh flowers for the table to make our "nests" as wonderfully romantic as we can, so too is the guy working to stop a leak before it turns into the Nile in our kitchens.

I hate changing the oil in my car. I think it's a horrible waste of time and my car is constantly on the brink of seizing up at any moment because of my attitude. Because of that, I decided to consciously change my views of changing the oil as an act of romance. It's a way that my husband wants, and is willing, to take care of me, so I'm willing to consider it an act of passionate romance.

Maybe you hate paying the bills. Could you consider him Casanova for sparing you that task and give him ten romance points for doing so?

It's important that women broaden their definition of romance to include things that some men are good at. Some men may never excel or even comprehend what it is that we're looking for romance-wise. Before you give up on them completely, consider adding a few new categories to the spreadsheet. If he eagerly fixes a leak, balances the checkbook, or does other valuable tasks that perhaps you've been overlooking, consider expanding your definition of romance to include his more utilitarian style.

You can light your own candles. You can buy your own flowers. You can probably change your own flat tire, too. But if you don't wish to spend your time and energy doing the latter, let him score major romance points for doing something so helpful. You'll both be happier with your new, broadened definition of romance!

97.
Suck at Something Together

"All things are literally better, lovelier, and more beloved for the imperfections which have been divinely appointed."
—John Ruskin

Take a one-day class in something you both want to learn, but both equally suck at. Whether it's cooking, golfing, skiing, painting, or pumping iron, find a hobby you both stink at, and then have fun learning together exactly why it is that you're so terrible at it.

You'll find tons of listings for one-day classes (or weekly ones, if you have the time) in your city or county's parks and recreation guides or through your area's community colleges.

Sucking at something together is a great cure for the couple that tends to set unattainably high goals and makes themselves miserable in the process. Think of all the hours in the week you spend trying to be the perfect worker, the perfect mate, the perfect parent, daughter, son, sister, or brother. We may try to be the perfect athlete, or at least try to have the body of one.

Many of us spend an awful lot of time feeling bad about ourselves for not living up to our impossible goals. And then we take that frustration home and take it out on our mates (who also don't live up to our ideas of perfection).

The worst part of seeking perfection is that we lose our sense of humor, and that's when the game is really lost. Fortunately, a sense of humor can be recaptured by giving up your ideas about perfection and seeking "suckiness" together.

Take a class in windsurfing. You *know* you're no good at it. You know you're probably *never* going to be very good at it. Why are you attempting to learn? Because it's fun, and it's funny.

It's tougher than it sounds, too. Let's say you and your mate agree to take a painting class together because you've always wanted to learn, in spite of the fact that neither of you show the slightest aptitude or artistic ability. Sure, it's easy to laugh your way through your initial attempt at a watercolor landscape—but as you start noticing *other* classmates' pretty pictures, just watch your seriousness and unattainable goals and the habit of unfairly comparing your abilities to others' (maybe your mate's) start to creep back in. Perfection seeking is a tough habit to break.

Take the class just to have fun together, and mean it.

metaphysical romance

98

Aromatherapy for Romance

"Nothing awakens a reminiscence like an odour."
—Victor Hugo

Throughout history, the scents of oils and herbs have been used to create a mood or desired reaction. Aromatherapy is not only helpful in healing what ails you, it can be sensational in setting the stage for romance.

Several essential oils are even considered aphrodisiacs. At the very least, they create an ambience that says "yes" to love and blocks out stress.

There are several ways you can use essential oils in aromatherapy. My favorite is to use a ceramic vaporizer with a tea candle underneath. About a tablespoon of water and a few drops of your favorite essential oils will heat up and fill a room with a light fragrance when the candle is lit.

Among the essential oils considered most helpful when the desire is for romance and passion are:

- **Patchouli**—An exotic scent of India. Considered an aphrodisiac because of its earthy, musky scent.
- **Rose**—Long considered the ultimate scent of femininity, also considered a powerful aphrodisiac. The scent of a rose is considered an antidepressant. Very sensual.
- **Cedarwood**—Woodsy scent with a stimulating effect, probably why it's believed to have an aphrodisiac quality.

- **Ylang Ylang**—Very exotic tropical flower. Believed to induce euphoria, lift one out of depression, calm, and create strong sexual, romantic feelings.
- **Neroli**—Orange blossom. Relaxing scent with an indescribable mystery to it. Believed to evoke feelings of sensuality.
- **Cinnamon**—Among the "pumpkin pie" spices that put men (particularly) in the mood for love. Traced back to the Queen of Sheba as an important scent.
- **Jasmine**—Powerful aphrodisiac from India. Particularly romance-inspiring for women. Used as a means of wooing men for thousands of years. Cleopatra is said to have used the scent of jasmine to cast her spell on Marc Antony.
- **Basil**—Believed to allay mental fatigue, basil is from the mint family and has a stimulating effect on the mind. Great romance begins in the mind. Use basil to inspire creativity and wit.

Experiment with these oils, using them one at a time until you find the one that's right for you and your mate. Don't assume that men will only find the more woodsy or earthy smells more enticing. Just as man is drawn to woman, he may be mysteriously drawn to the scent of jasmine or orange blossom. Take the time to enjoy the scent thoroughly yourself, and then use its magic on one another!

99.
Find Your Feng Shui Love Zone

You've probably heard about feng shui, maybe even read about it. You know it has something to do with the Chinese art of placement, whatever that means. You could start placing little mirrors and wind chimes all over your house, or you could just skip the rest of the feng shui custom and get to the good stuff.

I learned what I know about feng shui from two well-known, classically taught feng shui experts. I am far from being a master myself, but I learned enough to be able to tell you how to fix the love section of your house or at least get you started.

Draw an aerial view diagram of your home. The front door should be down at the bottom of the page. Looking at the blueprint of your home, the upper-right-hand corner (in relation to the front door) is the love section. If your home is shaped like an "L", your love section is missing and that would explain a lot of your problems in the romance department.

You can "cure" this problem by adding some feature outside the home in that missing corner that attracts "chi" (or life force) and spiritually completes the home so that it's a perfect square or rectangle. Several things attract chi. A bird feeder that is constantly stocked with seeds will attract birds and chi. Outdoor lighting of a special tree in that corner would attract chi.

The problem may not be a missing love section, but bad interior design. If your love section happens to be in a messy office space, or the place where you keep the cat's litter box...bad news. Move the cat box, clean up the office, get rid of clutter, and include art that shows a happy scene or creates a happy feeling. Things in the love section should be placed in twos. Two plants. Two chairs, etc. The color red is believed to attract chi. But if you're not comfortable with red, pick a warm color that you feel comfortable with.

Feng shui is also about balance. Masculine and feminine should be present. So if you've got nothing but flowers and frills in a bedroom in your love section, the man may not feel too welcome. But a tiny change can make a huge difference, such as adding a piece of wood furniture. Wood is masculine. So is rock. Water and anything reflective is feminine. Ditto hanging panty hose.

Make sure that anything in the love section that's broken gets fixed. Have any chairs, desks, or beds there "face" the door.

Good feng shui is basically just good design. A few simple changes in the love section of your home just might transform your whole house from a cold, uninviting place to a veritable love shack! And remember, clean, uncluttered homes are always more conducive to romance.

If none of the above makes your home more romantic—move. I'm only half kidding. The true devotees of feng shui—like first generation Chinese Americans—would never dream of buying a home without first having the chi checked out and approved by a master. Some problems, like a less than ideal slope of the landscape or a back door that's directly across and visible from a front door, are really difficult and expensive to fix. A true devotee would not buy a house with that kind of feng shui problem.

But the good news is, most of us are *not* devotees. I seem to always find myself in a home with major chi issues, and I somehow have managed to keep my money from flushing down the toilet, my career chi from flying out the door, and my marriage happy and intact. Message: take feng shui with a grain of salt, but *do* have fun with it. Following the advice of the ancient art, you are sure to make your home a more comfortable place, if not a delicious den of romance.

100.
Zen and Romance

"Zen is a way of liberation, concerned not with discovering what is good or bad or advantageous, but what is."
—Alan Watts

Even Zen Buddhism has something to teach us about romance, though it's extremely difficult to find anything about romance in the classical teachings of Zen. But it's there if you look hard enough.

First, a few basics about Buddhism for the novice. On the most basic level, Buddha taught that life is fraught with suffering and that the only way to get past the suffering is to stop desiring "stuff," or more of anything in life, and become enlightened through right thought, right conduct, meditation, and ultimately wisdom.

Zen Buddhism is the spiritual school that says meditate, engage in right thought and right action, and you will gain enlightenment.

I have meditated on my marriage many times. You can call what I was doing prayer. You can call it deep thought. But since I'm not very good at the strictest forms of meditation, it's all the same to me. But what I get back from my meditations are simple and profound: work it out. Stay on course. The journey is what is important. You are taking on big, big stuff (like facing your own flaws and the flaws of another). Don't walk away from the task.

Obviously, not all Zen Buddhists are monks, living high up on a hill away from the grit of real life and relationships. Buddhist teachings encourage those who are married to cherish their partners. Buddhism also teaches that since suffering is the reality of life (through our own fault), we should not expect marriage to always be pleasurable.

Buddhism encourages us to get to know our partners more, and then more, and then more. Down to the very core. The Buddha teaches that at the core of each of us, there is only love. It's the stuff on top of the love that causes all the friction, all the problems in our lives, all the suffering.

Zen Buddhism also teaches that if we are to have loving relationships, we cannot be selfish and be just "takers." We must be givers. Indeed, we must give and receive equally, completing each other. Just like yin and yang, male and female perfectly in harmony, we can learn how to be good and supportive partners to each other.

Even romantic relationships are hard work, and I love what Zen Buddhism says about work. It's found in an ancient saying: *Before Enlightenment—chop wood, carry water. After Enlightenment—chop wood, carry water.*

Zen also offers some wonderful advice about the work we all do: don't operate in automatic, be in the moment. Zen teaches that while you're chopping wood or carrying water that you should really think about what you are doing and why you are doing it. Applied to relationships, we can really be in the moment when we write our lover a letter. Even if we're just picking up their shirts from the cleaners, think about what you're doing and why you're really doing it. Do it with awareness, with mindfulness. Experience the feeling of driving to the cleaners and picking up the shirts. It's the alternative to thinking, *He'd better notice I did this for him!* Take pleasure in doing something for someone.

Give for the sake of giving and feel how good it feels in the moment—even something as simple and mundane as folding the towels. Fold them with love.

You have the power to transform your world through deep thought and conscious loving. Try to love every moment of every day. And when you succeed in transforming your world and romantic relationship, when you feel *lighter* and happier, you get to do it all over again. Fold the towels again with love.

101.
Make Your Life Creative

"One must still have chaos in oneself to be able to give birth to a dancing star."
—Friedrich Nietzsche

Commit to living your whole life in a creative way. Romantically, spiritually, economically, intellectually reclaim it and realize that the only limit is your own imagination.

If you're unhappy with your life, change it. You'd be surprised how taking control by changing one or two little things can create the effect of changing your whole life. Stop following conventional wisdom and start listening to your own inner wisdom.

Think outside the box in your romantic life. If you keep doing the same things in the same ways, you're always going to get the same results. Look at the results you have right now and see if there's something about them that you'd like to change. Ask yourself what small thing you could do differently that might end up changing your whole outlook.

Creativity in your life can mean living the same life you're living now: the same career, the same home, obviously the same family, but approached in a slightly different way. It can simply mean riding a bicycle to the grocery store or coffee shop rather than taking your car. You'll be surprised how much more romantic your life can feel just by doing one thing that causes you to live more fully in the moment and experience life around you. Living your life creatively can mean taking your kids out for a twilight picnic. Kidnapping your husband at the end of his day and taking him camping is a creative way to change one weekend, and, eventually, everything you thought you knew about the way your life is going.

To commit to living your life creatively is to open up your mind to opportunities and new ideas all the time. It doesn't have to be hard work. Hard work is drudging along in a rut that offers no fun at all. Creativity, on the other hand, is very fun and does not have to mean work or "outdoing" the last creative thing you did. It's skipping a meeting that nobody really cares if you attend anyway and eating an ice cream cone on the sidewalk instead.

Take a look at your life and start jotting some things down in your journal. What is working for you and what is boring the heck out of you? Take some tiny risks.

Take a look at your relationship. Is there a routine or pattern you have developed that neither of you really enjoy? Open your mind to new possibilities.

The unfortunate thing about patterns and ruts is that they're so easy to replace—*with new patterns and new ruts!* You know what I mean. You decide that you have a rut of making love in the dark, so you turn on some dimmed lights. The next thing you know, you're making love in dimmed lighting every single time. A new rut!

So, when you commit to living your life creatively, don't sit down and laboriously come up with a list of one hundred things you could do differently if it means that you will never want to sit down and force yourself to come up with another list like that ever again. Just open your mind to possibilities and take a few daily mental notes.

This is the holistic approach to romance. Heal what's not working in your whole life and watch the romance start thriving again. Start living with an open mind. Ask the universe to send its creativity your way and allow fresh ideas to spring to mind.

You are the artist of your world. Paint it with joy and a fresh canvas every day.

102.

Be a Sexual Being

"A woman is a creature who has discovered her own nature."
—Jean Giraudoux

You are a multifaceted person. You may be a mother, a wife, a girlfriend, a friend, a daughter, a sister, an employee, a philanthropist, a child of God.

Each role you play demands certain things of you. And those demands can be so weighty, I think we sometimes try to pare down some of the ones we deem unnecessary or too low on the list of priorities. We might not do this on a conscious level, but I believe we do it just the same. The key is not eliminating any of those roles, but finding balance with all of them.

As women bogged down with the responsibility of all these roles, we may completely forget that we are also sexual beings. It was so easy to remember in early adulthood. Back then, we thought of ourselves as sexual beings every time we got dressed to walk out the door. Some looked sexy, some demure, others earthy, some athletic, etc. It was all a reflection of how we wanted to present our young woman selves to the world—fully aware that we were budding sexual beings.

As we got older, our sexual identity may have become even more important to us. We learned what kind of partners we liked, what we wanted from them, what turned us on, and how we could turn *them* on.

But as we became immersed in the role of "Career-Woman," or "Mom," or "Do-it-All-Home-Improvement/Decorator," it's possible that our vision of ourselves as sexual beings got shoved gently aside. Or that vision just faded away.

As sad as that sounds, the great news is that no matter how much you've denied your sexual nature, it's never left you. You're still a sexual being. The trick is to start thinking of yourself as such.

Just accepting that truth will probably be all that you need to do. When you accept that you're a sexual being, it's easier for you to recognize the moment when the kids are away from the house and the husband is home and see it as a perfect moment for romance. The woman who doesn't see herself as a sexual being might only think of that moment as a great opportunity to wash the floors, providing she can manage to lock her husband in the den so he won't track footprints.

When you recognize that of all your many facets, the sexual being facet is just as important as the rest, it becomes easier to recognize the time in your days and weeks that could be spent romantically.

Think of yourself as a diamond. Perfectly cut diamonds, with all their shimmering facets, are balanced. The beauty is in the balance. It's where the fire comes from. Without balance, there is no spark, nothing to catch the light. Each facet has a purpose and plays a part in supporting the shape of the diamond. The "sexual being" facet of you is as important as any other. Let it bring out the fire in you.

"Grow old with me! The best is yet to be!"
—Robert Browning

Take an evening together to create a simple collage, a collection of pictures that illustrate what your life together will look like in five, ten, or twenty years. Decide on a date in the future when the collage will accurately reflect your goals together.

Cut out pictures from magazines and glue them down on a piece of cardboard backing. Choose scenes that depict the place where you might like to live together. Find pictures of couples walking hand in hand on the beach at sunset. Put a real picture of the two of you now, looking happy together (hugging or kissing) right in the center of the collage. If travel is a major goal, cut out and glue pictures of airplanes, cruise ships, or trains that clearly depict that goal.

Include the way you'd like your life together to look materially (like a picture of a cute cottage you want to live in, or a houseboat), but be careful that your relationship, or, at the very least, the *taste* of romance and happiness are obvious in the collage. The reason I say that is because this visualization technique really *works*. If all you ask for through the pictures of your collage are material things like cars and boats and fancy houses, you'll get them, but that's *all* you'll get. The universe will silently answer, *You didn't ask for happiness. You didn't ask for romance or love. You asked for this stuff, and that's what you got!*

It's why the saying "be careful what you wish for" is so true. *Ask and ye shall receive* isn't just a quaint quote from the Bible, it's the actual gospel truth.

Because it's so true, you're very safe if you ask for happiness and let your collage reflect that ultimate goal.

I think a lot of people who believe in the powers of visualization assume that they need to take care of their material needs and the rest will follow. They believe that if you visualize wealth, you'll also get happiness. But the exact opposite is true. Visualize happiness, and when you get it, it won't come with your being in debt up to your ears or without enough food to eat. How could you be happy that way?

Create a collage that creates an impression of what you really want your life together to be about in however many years. Then, when you're finished, find a good pen and write in a key place in the collage "Our life together in the year ___." Put the collage someplace where you'll see it daily.

If you've really created a collage with pictures that you love, you'll have no trouble finding a minute or two a couple of times a week just sitting and staring at it (visualizing).

You don't have to visualize together, and you can even make separate collages if you wish. Just be sure you both have a happy picture of the two of you in your collages. You can dream about different material things, and it's fine to picture romance and love and happiness expressed in different ways. But if you picture entirely different things for your lives a few years down the road, this can also be a great starting point for a deep conversation about where you're headed as a couple.

We can't visualize things for other people, especially if they object to the vision. I may want to live on a remote island somewhere and devote my life to painting, but if my husband wants to live in the city and we're determined to stay together, someone's visualization is going to evaporate to a certain degree. It may be resolved by my getting just a vacation home on an island.

Whatever *slight* differences that may exist in two people's visualizations, the universe knows how to work them out. There is always a way.

A Girl's Best Friend

"Look for a lovely thing and you will find it.
It is not far—it never will be far."
—Sara Teasdale

f a diamond really is a girl's best friend, why not open yourself up to dozens more worthy acquaintances in precious and semi-precious stones and metals of the Earth? While some dismiss crystal power as ridiculous hocus-pocus, there are new-age scientists who firmly believe that certain gems carry the energy essences of everything we desire, including romance.

Almost every culture in the world has at some point used rocks, crystals, and minerals for spiritual reasons, weaponry, cooking, home-building, or reasons of the heart.

Stones have been used to ward off evil spirits, ensure fertility, and inspire and gain love. Crystals are mentioned in the Bible, found in the great pyramids of Egypt and the wondrous tombs of Chinese emperors.

Do stones and precious metals really have special powers? It's any-one's guess. A diamond, for example, may not really inspire purity and intensity of love, but I for one am willing to take that chance and selflessly load myself down with any old diamond given to me.

For the purposes of inspiring romance and passion, it's believed that special stones can be worn, placed on the body while meditating, or posi-tioned in areas of the home where you want the inspiration.

To learn a lot more about the new-age beliefs about crystals, check out *Love is in the Earth* by Melody. But just to get started, here are just a few of the stones and minerals believed to aid in the pursuit of romance, passion, and love.

- **Sardonyx**—Onyx with layers of carnelian. Makes you happier and easier for someone else to live with; makes you more joyful.
- **Orange Spinel**—Fertility aid, said to dispel frigidity.
- **Pink Tourmaline**—Pink is an important color in the shades of love. It's the color of the heart. Pink tourmaline is believed to give you faith in the power of love.
- **Diamond**—The stone most used in engagement rings, its purity, fire, and strength symbolize everlasting love. The diamond is also believed to attract good fortune to the wearer and inspire confidence and creativity.
- **Rose Quartz**—Long regarded as one of the kindest of the stones. It is believed to possess a loving nature and will help the wearer get in tune with a gentle love-force. Self love is also promoted by the rose quartz.
- **Emerald**—Believed to create domestic bliss and help love in every way. Helps partners be more sensitive.
- **Amazonite**—Aids with communication of the heart, soothing and rejuvenating.
- **Ruby**—Stimulates heart chakra and creates mental sharpness. Also considered a stone of amazing good fortune. Makes wearer more loving but also brilliantly "sharp."
- **Sodalite**—Helps couples make and achieve common goals.
- **Topaz**—Considered the stone of true love, replaces negativity with positivity.
- **Turquoise**—Helps one communicate feelings, inspire romance and romantic spontaneity. Considered a master healer, and very important in the Native American traditions.
- **Jasper**—Inspires one to remember that we are here on this Earth to care and love one another, not to be an island.
- **Barite**—Enhances harmony and love, creates intuition in matters of love.

- **Quartz Crystal**—Helps one meditate on a problem, bring a positive visualization into reality.
- **Moonstone**—Helps one's intuition. Helps wearer appreciate the cycles and seasons of relationships. Brings happiness and is the "wishing stone."
- **Copper**—Activates the base chakras, the sexual chakras. Increases sexuality, desire, vitality, but also seeks to create a beautiful balance.
- **Flame agate**—Stimulates passion and physical vitality.

Will your mate think you've lost your mind as you place little rocks and amulets around the house for good luck? Maybe not. A friend of mine who became interested in crystals just told her husband the rocks were the latest craze at the import store, and he questioned no further.

Crystals may not help your relationship, but they can't hurt either. And some of them are quite beautiful, anyway. If you decide to give crystals a try, remember that the experts believe that each rock is very special, so as you're selecting them, hold them in your hand and "feel" if they're right for you. What have you got to lose?

105.

Three Small Wishes

> *"Our desires, once realized, haunt us again less readily."*
> —Margaret Fuller

If you could get your spouse to dress up like a genie out of a bottle (good luck) and grant you three wishes, what would you wish for? What if the wishes were only good for one year, at which point you could ask for three brand new wishes?

One very happy couple I know says their whole marriage turned around after they created one simple annual ritual just like this (minus the dressing up in genie harem-wear). Once a year, they check in to a nice hotel and bring with them a lovely bottle of wine. They get comfortable in their hotel room and start sipping on their wine. Then they ask each other the magic question.

"If I could grant three wishes for you over the next year, what would they be? What could I do for you?"

Sarah and Jonah are free to ask for anything. Sometimes the wishes are as simple as 1) Give me three minutes of your undivided attention when you get home from work. 2) Make love no fewer than twice a week. 3) Plan one nice, two-week vacation for us this winter.

Other years, the wishes require more effort: 1) Treat me especially kindly in front of your mother. 2) Don't raise your voice when we're arguing. 3) Help me establish a date night once a week.

Sarah and Jonah don't debate or argue over the other person's wishes.

They don't let wishes feel like criticism about things done or not done. They just toast to the wishes and promise to give it their best shot at making them come true.

They also go over last year's wishes and review whether they were ultimately granted or not. They talk about why some wishes didn't work out. Sometimes wishes are requested again. But again, there's no arguing about it. No blame. No guilt. No defensiveness.

Maybe it's easier for this ritual to be fun rather than a springboard for arguing because Sarah and Jonah make caring for one another a top priority. They also give each other a lot of trust, trust that the other is equally committed to being caring. That means if a wish of Sarah's doesn't come true, she never assumes it's because Jonah doesn't love her enough. She knows there's a good reason. Things happen. The goal isn't to be perfect, just to try a little harder.

The ritual also gets easier over the years. Jonah and Sarah say it changed their marriage, but it didn't happen overnight. Little by little, as small wishes get granted, they feel more loving toward one another and more forgiving and understanding when things aren't perfect.

The tiniest bit of effort shown as he walks through the door and remembers to give her three minutes of his undivided attention means so much and goes so far in convincing her that, *Hey, he really does care about how I feel.* Then, those small displays of devotion remind her to reciprocate as she's reminded, *Oh, yes, he'd really like for the newspaper to not be destroyed before he gets to read it.*

Isn't it funny that when we really think about what most in the world we would like to have, it almost always comes down to very little simple things?

The little details that Sarah and Jonah incorporate into their three wishes ritual shouldn't be overlooked if you're thinking about starting this ritual on your own. Sure, you could plan a special night at home instead of at a hotel room—but it's easier to get in another frame of mind in a place other than your own home. Being in a nice hotel room and sipping on some choice wine goes a long way in achieving a spirit more conducive to romance and agreement and less conducive to arguing or doing chores.

It should also be noted that Sarah and Jonah's ritual has been successful because they don't ask for wishes that are loaded, ambiguous, or negative, like "Stop being so cheap!" Jonah doesn't ask for Sarah to be "nicer" to him. Sarah doesn't ask for Jonah to be "more affectionate." The wishes have to be specific, like *Rub my feet once a week,* or *Always kiss me good-bye.*

With this ritual, the *worst* you can do is get a night every year in a plush hotel room with a nice bottle of wine. The *best* you can do is end up with a totally transformed marriage like Sarah and Jonah's: happier, more loving, more understanding—more romantic!

106.
Moon the New Moon Together

"Anyone can be passionate, but it takes real lovers to be silly."
—Rose Franken

arb and Alan have a special ritual they've built around the arrival of the new moon. They moon it. They mark their calendar together so that they know about each night that the moon begins a brand new cycle.

They see the night of the new moon coming with great anticipation. On the night of the new moon, they spend the evening at home, drinking beer and watching movies together. When darkness has completely fallen and they begin to run out of beer (whichever comes first), they run out to a fairly private part of their backyard deck and moon the new moon. They think of it as their little bottoms-up salute to the wonders of the cosmos. Then they run giggling back inside.

It's a really childish ritual. It's silly. And it's perfect for them. Barb and Alan think it's hysterical, and they look forward to it every time.

Says Barb, "The act has *some* actual significance, because we both are kind of spiritual and in awe of the cycles of the moon. And we wanted, as a couple, to honor the special night of the new moon in some way, and then it hit us: We should moon it! What would be a better tribute?"

It's also a great illustration of how rituals for couples don't have to be expensive.

Create a ritual for yourself, like Barb and Alan have, that makes you feel young, crazy, and in love. You may even want to adopt this goofy ritual for yourself until you find another one that has some kind of significance to you and your relationship. Until then—bottoms up!

Do a Grape Cluster

*"A rock pile ceases to be a rock pile the moment
a single man contemplates it, bearing within
him the image of a cathedral."*
—Antoine de Saint-Exupèry

A good friend of mine, nationally acclaimed personal coach Don Clarkson, swears by the "grape cluster" technique as a type of visualizing that's most effective in helping his clients get whatever it is they desire, be it more romance, a baby, even a vintage banana-cream-colored Mercedes-Benz 450 SL with beige-leather interior. Whatever you want, Don says a grape cluster can help you get it.

I especially trust Don on this advice because in addition to being a personal achievement coach, helping hundreds of clients across the country knock down the roadblocks that stand in their way to success, he's also frighteningly psychic. I can't tell you how many times I've laughed off predictions about my life (like the one about my writing a book), only to feel dizzy when I see them come true before my eyes. So when Don tells me that romance-starved women everywhere can benefit from this obscure visualization technique, I believe him.

The "grape cluster" technique comes from a Hawaiian metaphysical approach called Huna. "Huna says that around any desire we may have is a cluster of smaller desires and images all connected to the greater cluster," Don instructs.

To do a grape cluster, take a piece of paper and in the center write down what you now believe to be your end goal—like more romance in your relationship. Around your central goal, start jotting down all your little goals and dreams related to the central goal. Things like: "I feel more loved," "I feel more cherished," "Moonlit walks on the beach," "Adding magic to my life," "Not feeling so alone, feeling part of an important unit," "I'd get more unexpected flower bouquets," "I'd get a date night, with my lover's undivided attention, at least twice a month."

You get the picture: create a little bubble for whatever your personal visions of romance are and reasons for wanting more of it in your life. Don't edit your wants. Make them all OK for you to desire.

Once you feel like you've written down all your little desires (grapes) around the big central desire, take a look at what you've written. Evaluate it objectively and make sure that all the little desires add up to the central desire. You may discover that it's not really more romance that you're after at all, just more communication, or time alone with your mate. Maybe what you're really after is more vacations or long weekends away from the pressures of home. The more accurate and clear you are about what it is that you actually desire, the better your chances of making it a reality.

Once you become clear, visualize your central desire and all your little desires as vividly as possible. Try to experience it as if it were happening now. Imagine a happy picture of what life looks like when all the little "grapes" have materialized.

"The grape cluster can bring from the subconscious to consciousness whatever one considers to be romantic, and from there the person can choose one image that she visualizes, and that process can often make the end result appear," explains Don.

Don teaches his clients that the subconscious has no idea what is real and what is imagined, so if you can create a vivid "real" picture in your mind that includes all your senses, the subconscious will believe it to be true and will help you make it happen.

Can visualization help someone make their partner more sensitive and loving? It can, says Don, but he also recommends to his clients the less metaphysical method of communicating to your partner exactly what you are in need of romantically.

Having done the grape cluster already, you've already taken the first step, which is getting clear on exactly what it is that romance means to you, and what it is that you desire more of. Then, share your notes with your lover.

"It's important that a couple be on the same page in terms of definitions, and that's the trickiest part," says Don. It's not enough that you ask him to be more romantic, or give him only one example of how you'd like that romance to be manifested. He won't get the full picture without seeing your grape cluster and understanding that it's about much more than just coming home with flowers every six months.

Finally, Don asks his clients to be sensitive to the true meaning of love. It's great to want more romance, but equally important that you give as good or better than you get:

> Most of us are very concerned about what the other person is, or should be, doing for us. Love is an active verb, meaning it's something you *do*, not something you *get*. I might ask a client what *she* has done lately that is romantic in the hope that her partner would get the message and do more romantic things in return. If he doesn't, perhaps there is more of an issue in the relationship than just romance.

In any good relationship, you both work to make each other's dreams come true. But first, you have to have the *dream,* the discovery of what exactly it is that your heart desires.

*"Prayer is the contemplation of the facts of life
from the highest point of view."*
—Ralph Waldo Emerson

I believe wholeheartedly that prayer should be included at the beginning, middle, and end of every problem. If romance, or the lack of it, is a problem in your life, prayer can help. Nothing is too great or too trivial for God, whatever your conception of God may be.

Is it ridiculous to pray for help with romance? I don't think so. How to ask God for help? You could start by inviting spirituality to dwell within your relationship. You could just ask for help. Ask humbly and with an open heart.

But what are we really asking for when we ask for God to help us with romance? Are women really praying for men to remember to buy us flowers on special days? Of course not.

When we pray for romance, we are really praying that the magic and mystery of love continues to dance between our partners and ourselves. We are bowing to the mystery of the love that we share with each other.

Romance is a pathway and a playground for something much deeper, the truth about ourselves and our purpose on Earth: to love.

One of the most talented and insightful writers on prayer is Marianne Williamson. In her book *Illuminata: A Return to Prayer,* Williamson warns people not to give up on a relationship once the romance fades. She believes that only when the initial passion fades do we have an opportunity to move on to something deeper, truer, and just as passionate but for different reasons. Williamson suggests that we should pray for the truth about our relationships.

If you have little experience at prayer, but are open to it, I urge you to read any of Williamson's books. The good news is that you don't *need* any special instruction when it comes to prayer. Just open your heart and speak.

Prayer has helped my marriage through times when nothing else could. All couples go through tough stages that are like gateways—times when you're ready to enter another level, but there's friction getting there. A lot of people give up before they ever get to a new and exciting level.

Thank God I didn't. At a point when we were experiencing the most friction, we took what was supposed to be the romantic trip of a lifetime. Paris, the French Riviera, Italy: a marriage counselor couldn't have made a better prescription, or so we thought.

We fought in the rain in Paris, bickered through Nice, nearly parted in Portofino, and trashed each other through Tuscany. All I could think of doing was praying. Very convenient, because we were visiting something like ten cathedrals or ancient chapels every day. At every church, I offered my coins and lit a candle for my worries.

In those two weeks, I must have lit two hundred candles before different images of Mary (even though I'm not Catholic, this gave me a consistency that felt comforting to me). I imagined all the women over hundreds of years who must have stood in the same place I did, praying for the very same thing.

Each time I lit a candle, I imagined the smoke and the prayer drifting all the way up to Heaven. Hours after I left the candles, I pictured the flames and my prayers shining on. I thought of them as I toured the Louvre alone and walked through Ville Franche Sur Mer alone. My husband was off somewhere, probably as upset about everything as I was.

A week after my intensive prayer ritual began, in a tiny mountaintop village in Tuscany, Gary and I looked at each other and promised to work it out, to stop judging and start loving. Really loving. My prayers were answered.

When all seems hopeless, give prayer a chance. You never know what might happen.

ambience

109.
Rock and Romance

Getting back to *romance* is really about getting back to the important things in your life. It's about paying attention, being creative, slowing down and smelling the roses.

One of the best ways to slow down is to employ the evening ritual of rocking on a porch together and watching the world calm down for the night. I don't really have the right place for rocking chairs at my home, but I did manage to give new life to a totally useless area just outside my home by hanging a porch swing. It's gone from an ugly, purposeless part of my home to an area we treasure and use. It was one of the keys to making my house a haven for romantic living.

One beautiful home in my neighborhood doesn't have a front porch, but I noticed the residents added a beautifully built, self-supporting swing for two out in the middle of the front yard with a Plexiglas rain hood. It sits surrounded by their lovely landscaping. What a creative way to capture the essence of the front porch without undertaking an expensive and complicated addition.

Whatever you add, whether it's just rocking chairs or a grand wraparound, Southern-style porch, make a ritual of using it every week if not every day. Make it the place where you continue dinnertime conversations or the place where you catch up if busy family members missed dinner altogether.

Serve lemonade or iced tea on the porch. Have a glass of wine and talk peacefully with your lover. Make it a ritual that you talk about *pleasant* things while rocking or swinging on the front porch. You can fight later. You can vent about all your problems and gripes some other time. But make the moments on your front porch times made exclusively for happiness.

110.

Make Your Bedroom an Oasis

"Beauty of style and harmony and grace and good rhythm depend on simplicity."

—Plato

Keeping the whole house neat, vacuumed, and polished may be little more than fantasy for many of us, save for the rare moments when company is coming or the mother-in-law is scheduled to make her annual inspection. Busy homes are hard to keep up with, but you *can* maintain one small, perfect, clutter-free oasis from the chaos—in the bedroom.

If the bedroom is ever going to serve as the most romantic room in the house, if it's ever going to be a place where you can relax easily and get in the mood for love often, then it is going to have to be pared down in stuff and piled high with sumptuousness.

The bedroom is a place that should be free from any kind of mail, bills, computers, and reading material that is for anything other than pleasure. It should be the one place where nothing stacks up or accumulates or makes its last stand before being ushered out to the garbage heap.

The bedroom is a place that should be treated to fresh air and ritual dusting. You can decorate it any way you like, so long as it is pleasing to you and soothing to the eye and spirit. It's a place in the home where, during a romantic moment, you are highly unlikely to get distracted by finances, work demands, kids' needs, or home-improvement necessities. If your whole house needs new carpeting or floor refinishing, *start* in the bedroom.

It goes against all the prevailing stupidity that usually accompanies home decorating, remodeling, and organization. Most people (like me, until I learned my lesson) make the bedroom the last priority in the house because guests won't see it.

But we're starting to see decorators and homeowners finally turn the bedroom into a priority. Lisa, a cousin of mine, seemed like a renegade revolutionary when she recently took this approach to remodeling her home, stupefying everyone who visited and every "expert" enlisted in the task. She and her husband were restoring a turn-of-the-century home that had suffered hideous updates over many decades. While the rest of the home stood for a few *years* in various states of reconstruction ruins, Lisa made sure her bedroom and bathroom got finished to a high, beautiful gloss right away.

"I knew this project was going to last forever and that it would be chaotic. I just wanted to have one area of my home that was *finished*. A place where I could escape to and relax and pretend the rest of the house looks just like this," she explained to perplexed visitors, unaccustomed to hearing such practicality and common sense in the arena of remodeling.

Most people will do just the opposite in a home-improvement project (and for many of us, our homes are *constantly* in a state of transformation). Oftentimes, if the homeowners can only afford to make repairs one step at a time, they'll start by improving the high-visibility places, like the living room and kitchen. Then they'll gradually (read: *never*) make their way to the low-visibility spots, such as the master bedroom.

Using this approach, the master bedroom can easily end up being the room with the ugliest carpet, the cheapest furniture, and the piles and piles of clean, unfolded laundry and stacks of bills and clutter. The front rooms stay spotless, just in case the President and First Lady drop by for coffee. Meanwhile, the room that's supposed to be the most relaxing, restful, and romantic in the house becomes a habitat of headaches.

If the above accurately describes the room in your home where you rest your head every night, give it a makeover and a new lease on life and romance. Clean it up! Clear it out! Cleanse your spirit and make way for romance and relaxation!

The Best
Wind Chimes Ever

"Music can be translated only by music."
—Oliver Wendell Holmes

I know you're going to think I'm crazy, that I've *fenged* one too many *shui*. But when it comes to outdoor ambience, and a smooth, subtle, romantic, even haunting sound that can be heard inside the home, you need wind chimes. And not just any wind chimes, but the best wind chimes ever, which I have been lucky enough to find.

If you can find a part of your home that gets a gentle breeze, having wind chimes hanging is like having a different romantic song playing all the time without wasting electricity or having to change the CD.

I know, you're thinking, *Wind chimes?* Those things that go clinkity-clank and never shut up? Trust me. The kind of wind chimes I'm talking about you have never heard before and won't be able to live without after you do.

The right wind chimes are like the sounds of pure romance and magic dancing on the wind. Perfectly hand-tuned, they play light, gentle songs that are hypnotizing and belong on everyone's front or back porch, right next to the rocking chairs or porch swing. Wind chimes mask the unromantic sounds of traffic and the too-close neighbors.

You're looking for a serious, musical set of wind chimes, such as those I found from Grace Note Windchimes (www.gracenotewindchimes.com). Make sure you're buying hand-tuned, musical wind chimes and you won't go wrong.

Buy one, and you'll be so pleased you're sure to buy more. I now have six—four big ones and two little ones. And I want *more!* They bring a peaceful, romantic feeling every time the breezes blow.

112

Romantic Gardening

*"Blossoms are scattered by the wind and the
wind cares nothing, but the blossoms
of the heart no wind can touch."*
—Yoshida Kenko

When I think of romantic gardens, I picture billowing, bursting English cottage gardens. Roses and wisteria climbing and twisting around doorways and gates. I picture white shasta daisies and black-eyed Susans and French lavender. I see gracefully arching mimosa trees creating shade for romance and escape from the blazing sun.

The only trouble with this vision is that this type of garden is an awful lot of work. I know; I have a garden just like it right outside the office where I'm now writing.

They look great in magazines, but when you recreate them in real life it's mind boggling how much time is required for weeding, pruning, watering, etc. You're never finished and there's no time for the white linen dresses and peaceful retreats on a garden bench with mint juleps.

But in my years of gardening and watching my very English grandmother and my aunt, I have learned a thing or two about creating a romantic English garden without breaking the bank, your back, and saving a little time for things like romance—or, in my Grandma's case, tea.

If you're creating a romantic garden from scratch, my advice is to find a tiny portion of your yard where you can design a little "setting."

Don't focus on the whole yard unless you're really prepared to go nuts for the next eight years while you're planting and waiting for the plants to fill out.

Find a tiny space and set it apart from the rest of the yard so it's at once an outdoor retreat and a place that looks like its own space. You can set apart your tiny romantic garden with a short, white picket fence surrounding it. You can do it with hedges or boxwoods. There's no end to the possibilities; it's all a matter of personal taste.

Once you've decided on a little space where your romantic garden will be, hire someone to do the back-breaking work of sod removal and shoveling in compost or better soil. The rest is the fun part.

Decide where you're going to put a bench or a table and two chairs within the setting. You can cover the ground there with pea gravel or something more formal if you wish.

Now that you have the space defined, go nuts with planting. Start with actual plants, not seeds.

In areas that get a fair amount of sunlight, plant roses, shasta daisies, lavender, grasses, purple coneflowers, daylilies, and coreopsis. Plant only a few feet apart to create an English "overgrown" look.

Save yourself hundreds of dollars by begging gardener friends of yours to give you offshoots or parts of their favorite plants that need to be divided. Borrow their books on gardening and enlist their help in creating your tiny romantic garden. Most gardeners *dream* about doing an instant gratification, smaller garden project—they'll probably be happy (or just nosy enough) to help out.

The last secret of romantic gardening is to cover the remaining soil in between plants very carefully with bark mulch. Bark helps retain moisture and inhibits weed growth. So does overplanting. The more plants you have covering the dirt, the less opportunity a weed has to sneak in. Less time weeding, more time for romance!

The great thing about a small romantic garden is that it's a place to go and feel romantic all by yourself. The goal isn't necessarily to create a spot where you can lure your mate. My husband likes sitting on a garden bench for about six minutes max. But that's OK. The romantic garden is a place for *me*. It's *my* romantic oasis. A place for me to read, daydream, set goals, use my laptop, or just watch the birds.

Creating a romantic garden like this is really about creating a new room that's an extension of your home. It's a room that has the stars for a ceiling and flowers for a carpet. It has leaves for wallpaper and birds as noisy neighbors.

Take a walk around your yard or patio and see for yourself if you have the setting and the interest in creating a romantic garden space just for you—or for two!

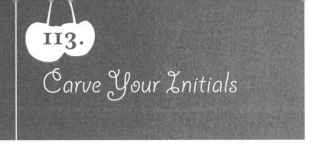

113

Carve Your Initials

"Bliss in possession will not last;
Remembered joys are never past."
—James Montgomery

Indulge in the old-fashioned practice of carving your initials someplace where you can revisit the carving forever. It's not just for puppy lovers, but for all who are young at heart and in love.

A word to the wise, though. Don't carve your initials in a tree since it will make the tree it vulnerable to disease and insects. Find a post or a pole (I have a special fence post in mind on my property) or even a piece of wood furniture like a porch swing and carve his initials + your initials. If you have never carved anything in your life, consider just using some outdoor paint and sealant to create your special message...no sense in severing a digit for love.

Why carve or paint your initials? First of all, to behave like young lovers. Second, for nostalgia. Every time you see your initials, you'll think of the moment when you put them there and remember how much in love you felt at the time. It's proof of love.

Another great idea is to plant a tree together on a special date you're celebrating, like your wedding or anniversary. As you water and nurture the tree, you remember how much care a relationship requires, too. As the tree grows, you watch your love and life together growing, too. It's a place to come back to. Someday, the tree will be tall enough to sit under together and relax in the shade.

Whether you're planting a tree or carving your initials, the idea is to create signs of love all around you. Symbols of love can counteract some of the stress in your life and remind you of what's good and special about it.

114.
Big Box of Romance

When I hired a personal organizer to come into my home and help me create some kind of organizational system for all my stuff, I rediscovered the vast array of things I had that could create a romantic setting. I had candles of every shape and size, romantic room fragrances, incense, you name it.

There was only one problem: all these critical things to create a romantic setting were scattered all over the house. In shoeboxes here, dresser drawers there, coat closets on another floor. With *that* kind of disorganization, it would take me two hours to gather all the stuff I'd need to create ambience for a special night. It would take my husband the better part of a month.

My organizer helped me to get all my romantic ambience stuff into a couple of boxes in the same closet. That way, my husband and I will have an easy time creating the mood in an instant, which is great for little surprise dates. Now, my husband can surprise me more easily and less expensively. Before I got this stuff organized, he'd either skip the ambience altogether or go out and *buy* new items (usually limited to candles in his case) *every time*. I'd do the same thing—only with a more broad array of accouterments. No wonder I have sixteen vanilla spice room fragrances and 170 candles!

Time to get organized. Ideally, according to my organizer, you would put your "big box of romance" somewhere in the same room where you'd primarily use the stuff. So, probably a closet in the bedroom would be ideal. If you have a locking cedar chest in your room, housing blankets that you never use, this could also be a perfect place.

No stuff to put in a big box of romance? Here are some shopping ideas to create your own.

- **Candles of every shape and size**—Buy them when you see them on clearance but make sure they're made in the U.S. or Canada or you could expose yourself to harmful chemicals.
- **CDs of your favorite romantic music**—Let's say music by Sting just turns you on, but you already have all his CDs. Get duplicates to keep in your box. If you've got ten minutes to get ready for a romantic hour or two, you don't want to spend it tearing up the house and going through your car, desperately searching for your favorite CDs.
- **Room fragrance**—This sounds crazy, I know, but go for food smells like pumpkin pie spices and apple pie spice (both have a strong cinnamon smell). Studies have shown that men are most turned on by fragrances of the pumpkin pie variety, even if they don't like the taste of pumpkin pie!
- **A very skimpy nightie**—Enough said.
- **A ladies' razor and shaving cream**—For last-minute leg grooming.
- **Pink light bulbs**—In case you want more light than the candles provide. Pink, of course, is the most flattering of colors for indoor illumination.
- **Massage oils, lotions**—Just on the off chance that you have a little extra time to pamper one another.
- **Optional Toys**—I'll leave this area up to you and your imagination.

If you don't have things like candles or room spray handy, you'll never use them, and they really can add a lot to a romantic moment. Keeping them in a single box will make it so much more likely that you or your partner can create a perfect romantic ambience quickly and easily. And ambience *is* important.

115.
Hire Someone to Serenade You

*"[Music] takes us out of the actual and whispers to us
dim secrets that startle our wonder as to who we are,
and for what, whence, and whereto."*
—Ralph Waldo Emerson

f your husband or boyfriend serenades you already, put this book down and email me, detailing exactly what you did to get him to do it (or where you found him and if he has a brother).

There aren't many things more romantic than the serenade—a man or woman playing the guitar and softly singing up to the window above.

But most of us can't play the guitar very well, and as for our singing voices, well, forget it. But that doesn't mean you can't still enjoy the serenade. All you have to do is call your local musician's association or union and hire one. Pay in advance through the association so that you don't have to spoil the mood by grabbing your checkbook. Have them come to your house and surprise your lover with a serenade in the middle of dinner.

It's a win-win. He gets a romantic surprise. You get serenaded by a guy who can actually sing.

"You can stroke people with words."
—F. Scott Fitzgerald

*P*ost-its are annoying. Voice mail and email are avoidable. Pieces of paper get lost in stacks of bills and clutter your space. The best way to remind each other about the love you feel (besides saying it aloud) is to get a "romance board," a small chalkboard placed somewhere where you can't miss the message on it and are always happy to see it.

A romance board is a great way to leave a note that simply says, "I love you." But try not to turn it into just another "to-do" or "honey-do" list; save those for the Post-its. The romance board is for communication that's pleasant, loving, *romantic*!

A romance board can be used to wish your partner good luck when you know they have an important presentation or pitch to make that day. It can be used to say "Happy Birthday," "Happy Anniversary," or to announce that you're cooking his favorite dinner that night.

A romance board has become essential in my marriage, since our work schedules sometimes have us going days without seeing one another. I want Gary to know that even though we won't see each other until Saturday (unless you count the sleeping hours), I'm thinking of him and love him.

A romance board is essential for the mate who is a frequent business traveler. It's a great place to leave a note that a loved one will see every day that you're gone. Just a simple message that says, "You're the love of my life; I can't wait to see you on Thursday. I'll be thinking about you the whole time," would be so nice for the lover at home, waiting.

Colored chalk makes the messages even more fun. Of course, once you have fun chalk and a chalkboard handy, your kids, if you have kids, will be all over it. No one can resist a clean chalkboard and chalk in every color of the rainbow. That's why I ended up having to have *two* chalkboards. One for the kids, one just for us.

If you're having a tough time thinking of ways to work more romantic messages into your relationship, if you're tired of the phone and endless email, consider something more personal. A romance board can become a beautiful part of your home surroundings, a great way to reconnect and send thoughts of love every day. A romance board out in plain sight will catch the eye of visitors who'll see your messages of love to each other— but who cares? Maybe you'll inspire them to be more loving, too.

117

Say It with Flowers

*"The flower is the poetry of reproduction. It is an
example of the eternal seductiveness of life."*

—Jean Giraudoux

Did you know that the oleander is the flower of warning? Or that the tuberose means "dangerous pleasure?" Did you know that if someone hands you a hyacinth, right-side up, it means "Please forgive me," while someone handing you lemon blossoms, upside down, signifies infidelity?

It's all part of the language of flowers, interpreted and reinterpreted through religious tradition for thousands of years, but more recently put down in book form by Victorians.

The first to start the formal tradition of "floriography" was Mademoiselle Charlotte de la Tour, whose book *Le Language de Fleurs* became an immediate bestseller in 1819. Then came the true experts of the late 1800s. Miss Corruthers of Inverness's definitions stand as the genuine authority, even today. They are probably responsible for the fact that nothing says love quite like a single red rose, which means "love, pure and simple."

One of the reasons why floriography was so important to the Victorians is that the repressed society simply would not permit them to express their true feelings in any other way. If they wanted to say to a man, "You are my secret love," they'd say it by handing him a simple acacia stem.

It makes me wonder how learned the *men* of those times were on the subject of floriography. Did they really know what they were being told when a young woman casually handed them peach blossoms (that symbolically mean, "I am your captive")? Probably not; I'm guessing it was entirely a women's sport and men relied heavily on the education and insight of the other women around them to get a clue.

Today we've got perfect freedom of speech. Maybe there's too much speech, though. Wouldn't it be nice to get a secret message once in a while? You'd know that someone had "a special message" for you if they gave you an iris or a nightshade. (I would really not recommend giving a friend nightshade though, since their cat might eat it and then drop dead. It's highly poisonous. Then they'll be sending you basil, which means, "I hate you. You killed my cat!")

Just as it's intriguing to hear of couples who've developed their own little cues at parties (tug of the ear means "lets go make out in the car!"), I think it would be very romantic to delve into the supposed meanings of flowers. Wouldn't it be fun if he sent you a bouquet with four kinds of flowers whose meanings added up to "Beware..." (oleander), "...your purity..." (lily), "...is in danger!" (rhododendron), "I'm transporting you to ecstasy!" (gardenia).

Admittedly, that might make one *ugly* flower arrangement (rhodies and gardenias together?), but the important thing would be that it had a *secret message* that it might take you hours to figure out!

This is something that *even he* might think is romantic and fun, if you started it first by sending *him* flowers and letting him know that there's a secret message and he'd better do a search on "floriography" on the Internet if he wants to know what you're telling him.

Let's say you've just found out you're pregnant, something he's been waiting and hoping for. A bouquet of iris ("message"), verbena ("may you get your wish"), and palm ("victory") would do the trick. (But I'd also hide a pacifier or a diaper pin down in the foliage just in case he gets stumped.)

There's no doubt flowers are just plain romantic. Floriography can be good romantic fun, even if you're the only one who knows the secret (a bouquet of tulips, meaning "I declare war on you!" to your husband's new, pretty assistant). But it should be pretty easy to get girlfriends in on the game as you send them zinnias ("thoughts of faraway friends") or oak ("thanks for the hospitality")—though I can't really offer any thoughts on how to make a bouquet of oak look like a nice gift.

Hidden meanings are fun. And no one can accuse a Victorian of being unromantic. (Frigid, yes. Unromantic? Never!) A true Victorian woman knew that saying something in a secret language, just the mystique of it, instantly created more romance and interest. How could she fail in gaining a man's affections when instead of bombarding him with words, she handed him a lilac? His sister would later tell him that the lilac symbolizes "the first, true love."

When in doubt, or when you just want to make what you have to say more mysterious and romantic, say it with flowers.

118

Indulge in Seasonal Rituals

"I should like to enjoy this summer flower by flower,
as if it were to be the last one for me."
—André Gide

There are so many romantic ways you can enjoy each season, ways you can celebrate the arrival of the seasons of
each new year of your life together. Watch your love grow as you experience the world renewing itself with the first snowfall, the budding of
spring leaves, birds building nests, and trees changing colors.

What I love about many seasonal rituals is that they force you to really
be in the moment. That's not true for all of the rituals. You can buy
Christmas presents months in advance and not really get into the spirit of
it. But if you take a drive to go look at the fall colors, you have to be there
to enjoy it. You have to take it all in then and there. You can't wait a few
more weeks to enjoy it because it will all be gone and the opportunity lost.
It's a ritual you have to seize and enjoy with all your heart. After all, how
many autumns do we get to see in one lifetime? Not so many that we can
afford to let one sneak by us unnoticed.

Autumn is my new favorite season to celebrate. I don't know why I
overlooked it all my life. It doesn't have the glitz and glamour of winter. It
doesn't have the sizzle of summer. It doesn't have the newness of spring-
time. But I now think autumn is the best time of year. It's not terribly cold
yet, but just cold enough to start lighting fires again, start pulling out cud-
dly sweaters. It has the most dramatic colors that nature offers. The

weather can still be warm during the daytime, but it cools way down at night, making it a perfect time for snuggling beside a fire.

119

Buy Your Fantasy Bed

"Our truest life is when we are in dreams awake."
—Henry David Thoreau

Our bedrooms are supposed to be the most romantic rooms in the house. And the bed, of course, is the focal point of that romantic space. We spend a third of our lives in bed; shouldn't it be the most wonderful, most romantic bed we can possibly find and afford?

My friend Stacey is definitely one who subscribes to the belief that every woman should have the bed of her fantasies. She was promised she'd get one as a consolation prize when her husband's job moved them across the country to a place where she knew absolutely no one.

They bought a pretty house, and for icing on the cake, her husband Dave (yes, the same Dave who inspired the chapter "Tinker With the Thermostat") took her to the furniture capital of the world, North Carolina, to decorate their new home.

She spent the day picking out some real treasures: tables, chairs, china hutches—you name it. It was every woman's fantasy shopping trip. Dave was agreeable to all of it, right up to the moment when their salesperson was about to ring up the nine thousand dollar bed Stacey picked out. According to Stacey, Dave's response to the price tag could likely be heard by people in *South* Carolina.

Stacey was forced to "settle" with a bed that cost something like $4,500. Apparently it looks just like her original dream bed but isn't made of the same quality wood.

I was really lucky or maybe just have bad taste or possibly a combination of the two. My dream bed was relatively cheap. One Valentine's Day, I set out to find our perfect bed as a surprise for Gary (read: *me*, a Valentine's surprise for *me!*).

After shopping all day, and totally aghast by all the enormous, overdone, completely pretentious, *how-the-hell-do-you-even-get-something-that-big-into-your-house?* beds, I finally stumbled across something that was totally ME!

Picture off-white square-ish headboard and footboard in a Georgian style with a lot of detailing, all crackle and smudge finished to make it look like it had been around for about three hundred years in someone's attic. *I was in love!* Best of all, I found a floor sample being sold at a clearance price less than $1,500!

That was about four years ago, and I can honestly say I love the bed even more now than I did then. It's so romantic. So timeless. Even Gary loves it. I wake up every morning and almost always have a quick moment when I think about how much I love that bed. You really could bury me in it.

I can't see myself ever wanting another bed for the rest of my life. I conceived my first and second children in this bed. This is where Gary and I share stories and relive funny things that happened during the day.

This bed is where our romance and friendship are renewed, where we find a quiet moment, where we watch the lightning storms and stare at the ceiling, hoping our roof can make it a few more years. This bed is a member of the family!

If getting the bed of your dreams is something you're still planning on doing *someday*, take some steps to start making it happen today. Go out and find it, then do what it takes to create a financially responsible way of bringing it home: layaway, credit union loan, have a garage sale and raise money for it, whatever you have to do to start making that dream (if it *is* a dream to you) a reality.

The bed is a very important place when it comes to romance. Make yours special to you. Get the bed of your dreams.

120

Set the Mood with Candles

"A mighty flame followeth a tiny spark."
—Dante Alighieri

Candles are the easiest, most inexpensive way to transform an ordinary room into a room made for romance. I like to have hundreds of candles handy in boxes where I can easily find them. But not all candles are created equal.

You don't have to buy the most expensive candles to create wonderful ambience, but you do need to follow one rule without fail: Don't buy a candle made in any country that doesn't have strict standards about candlemaking. More about that in a minute.

When shopping for candles, purity is important. Beeswax is best, but not critical. And unscented candles may be safer and less irritating than the scented kinds. If your candles seem to be giving off black smoke, that's a signal that the candle is not pure and should not be used inside the home.

My favorite color candles are orangey-yellow because, when lit, they give off a wonderful warm glow and share that warmth with the whole room. I think they create the perfect romantic ambience.

Candles in tins are best for the bedside and for travel because you don't have to worry about damaging surfaces or waxy drippings, and they're safer in case you fall asleep.

To get the best deals on domestically made candles, look for sales and then buy lots. You can get some of the best deals on candles at the really expensive decorating stores when they're holding clearance sales on out-of-season items. Right after the Christmas holidays is a great time to stock up on high-quality candles.

Teach your husband how to light a candle for ambience. Tell him how much you love the way a candle can change the mood of a room. Ask him to light candles for meals and turn the lights off. If he knows that it's going to make you feel sexier and more romantically inspired, he'll start collecting candles too and lighting them whenever he can. You might think that your love for candles is obvious to your mate because you light them all the time. But if you haven't told him *why* you love candles and how they can be used to create settings in which you'll automatically feel more romantic, he hasn't gotten the picture.

Men think that every conversation must serve some purpose with a clear goal in mind. If you tell him that you want candles lit more often to feel more romantic, he'll get it.

Now, an important word about candle producers. In the U.S., Canada, and most European countries, candle makers conform to certain rules and ingredients. Any time you buy a candle from another country that doesn't have extremely strict rules, you're taking a chance, with lead poisoning being a real danger. I know of people whose homes are contaminated with lead—all because of cheap, imported candles they used on a regular basis.

To make sure that you're buying a candle made in a "safe" country, look at the label on the bottom of the candle. If it doesn't list the place of manufacture, assume it's *not OK*. It's more expensive to make candles in the U.S. than in many other countries, so those candle makers are sure to brag about their domestic production.

You don't have to pay a fortune, but it's worth investing in pure candles that can transform an ordinary room into a romantic haven!

121.

Light Your Fire

"Fire is the most tolerable third party."
—Henry David Thoreau

There is nothing so romantic as a crackling fire in the fireplace with a chilly wind whipping outside while you and your lover snuggle, warming your toes and rekindling the passion. Americans are so enchanted with the fireplace, it's actually the third-most-desired amenity in a new home (I'm guessing right after indoor plumbing and a roof that doesn't leak).

Even when it's hot outside, you can still create the romantic illusion of a flickering fire in the fireplace. Just place loads of candles at different levels in the fireplace and light them with a very long match. With the flue open, it's probably the safest place to have a lot of candles burning anyway. Smoke and heat go up, air stays cleaner inside your home, and should a candle fall over or burn to the base, it's in a safe place and won't start a fire. These days, there are lots of fireplace inserts to hold candles at different levels. We bought a nice wrought-iron one for about sixty dollars, but I've seen them for as little as fifteen dollars.

With enough multilevel candles flickering, it really does seem like you've got a fire burning in the fireplace, and it provides all the ambience you need to make a night (or early morning) special and romantic.

If you live in an area where there's not a lot of concern about smog buildup in the winter months, live it up and enjoy the fireplace you've got and make having a fire going part of your special romantic ritual at home. If you happen to live in an area where fires are regularly restricted because of air-quality concerns and romantic fires are really important to you, consider investing in a wood-burning stove that's certified environmentally friendly.

For the regular fireplace, there are a few things to consider when buying fuel. While manufactured fire logs are easier to light and supposedly burn much cleaner than firewood, some people can't do without the real thing. If that's you, know your wood so that you can create the best, most romantic, and trouble-free fire. Experts say that hardwood firewood, such as oak, hickory, ash, and madrone, burn cleaner than soft wood, like cedar, pine, and fir. Seasoned wood with a moisture content of less than 20 percent burns a lot cleaner than green wood. Just ask your cordwood supplier for their seasoned hardwood.

Have your chimney inspected once a year and cleaned as necessary. Energy experts recommend that you close all the interior doors to the room with the fireplace and turn your thermostat down to fifty-five degrees. Crack a window in the fireplace-room to a half-inch or an inch wide. This will give you a constant supply of fresh air that feeds the fire and is healthier for your lungs.

Taking care of these little details will guarantee that you won't be tinkering with the fire but spending all your time in front of a blazing fire building romance.

section eight

romance
survival

122.

Spend a Few Minutes Kissing Every Day

"Away with your fictions of flimsy romance;
Those tissues of falsehood which folly has wove!
Give me the mild beam of the soul breathing
Or the rapture which dwells on the first kiss of love."
—Lord Byron

One minute, it's the most exciting thing in our lives, the best and most passionate way to get close to our new lover. The next minute, it's relegated to a few perfunctory pecks we give each other in the brief moments immediately preceding sex. What happens to kissing? Why does it get so unfairly demoted, and why do so many people believe it would take a miracle to revive real, passionate kissing in their relationships?

Cherie Byrd just may have the answers. As the owner of a Seattle school that offers classes in kissing and tantric energy, Cherie spends a lot of time teaching couples how to bring back kissing and take their relationships to new levels.

I wanted to learn more about Cherie's class. I was pretty intrigued seeing an ad for "Kissing School." Cherie invited me and my husband to participate in a day-long class or get some private kissing lessons. I was trying to decide which would be more embarrassing: a class where dozens of couples spend seven hours kissing in front of each other, or getting *privately* critiqued on my kissing style. In the end, I opted to just interrogate Cherie on the importance and basics of kissing.

"Remember how much fun it was to make out in high school?" Cherie asks. "Go there. It's simply allowing it to be there, without allowing other expectations to enter in. It's about kissing and *not* starting to think, OK—now I need to start moving on to second base."

Some experts I've talked to believe that a couple will report feeling much more closeness if they just spend a minimum of ten minutes a week kissing. It is, after all, ten minutes more than many couples spend kissing. But Cherie would like to see couples spend several minutes *a day* doing it.

"It doesn't have to be uninterrupted kissing. Just a few minutes here and there. Do it while you're cooking dinner! After you've chopped the vegetables, spend ten minutes in the kitchen kissing passionately. I promise you that your dinner will taste much better if you do!"

Cherie believes that people have a tendency to isolate kissing in their lives, and that's where they go wrong. If we make fiery kissing *a part* of our everyday lives, it will become second nature and will never go stale.

Many women believe it wouldn't be easy to get their men to buy into "just kissing" for several minutes a day (or a week, for that matter).

Cherie suggests, "Ask for a gift of ten minutes of red-hot kissing. It will always be more important to women than to men, but men have a feminine, sensual side too. If you ask for that gift, they'll give it to you."

Why do women crave it more than men? Perhaps we crave true intimacy more, and there's no doubt that really great kissing is a path to intimacy.

"The real problem is, we don't know how to be intimate. To feel vulnerable and naked is a sacred experience that's not taught. It's not modeled, and the only place we ever see it is in the movies."

What's so magical and romantic about kissing? Cherie teaches couples that while our anatomy has created this profound possibility for powerful sensations, with countless nerve endings around the mouth and tongue, it's ultimately important on a spiritual level:

> What you really want to do when you're kissing your lover is to kiss a little bit of their soul. I teach people to pay attention to their breathing. If you're taking deep breaths while kissing, there's a flow between you, an energetic flow. This is the call to intimacy: when

the walls come down, and you start to experience them directly and deeply. It's what we're all looking for.

Think about how you could bring more kissing into your relationship. Spending several minutes a day kissing your mate may seem impossible to squeeze in. You may want to start with Cherie's advice about bringing it into your life, rather than setting aside some time for *mandatory* kissing. For some couples, though, ten minutes of scheduled kissing would be a radical improvement from what's (not) happening now.

At the very least, shift your thinking so that you're consciously honoring this thing that happens between us called a kiss. It's not just for young lovers. It's for anyone who wants to reach a deeper union with the one they love.

123.

Plan Romantic Escapes

Everyone knows that one of the secrets to great romance is to escape, to get away for "overnighter" dates often. Everyone knows it, but so few couples actually stick to it. There are a thousand excuses, a million reasons why it can't be done. But isn't it funny that the couples who *just can't* are the couples who need it most?

The busier you are, the more hectic your schedule and your life, the more reason there is to say *Stop!* for one brief, but regular, overnight trip to nowhere.

All of the marriage experts I've interviewed over the years stress how important it is for couples to get away regularly. It's strange how few things these experts agree on, but this is clearly one of them.

All couples need to get away. For the women, it's particularly critical. Men have a wonderful gift that's unique to their sex. They know how to get in the mood anytime, anywhere. Not so with women. If women had this same gift, it would never be necessary to ever leave the house for a date of any kind.

An overnight date at home is too difficult for a woman. She kisses his neck, touches his shirt, and suddenly finds her mind drifting off to the pile of laundry stacked in the hamper. He tosses the pillows onto the floor to create an Arabian Nights impromptu fantasy setting. But once on the floor, she sees floor-level dust. Would he mind if she just, very quickly, ran the vacuum? Yes, he says, he would very much mind the interruption. Dining room table? Nope, needs dusting. Playroom? Definitely not; toys everywhere and not at all arranged the way she had planned when she bought the IKEA kids' deluxe organizing shelves. The den? Lord, no! That's where the bills are stacked.

Before he's able to find a place in the house that doesn't cry for cleaning, organizing, or auditing—the phone rings. It's the kids. They forgot something that's absolutely vital to their existence. A stuffed animal of a very particular kind. Would Mom please drive it over to Grandma's? Along with the blue spacecraft pajamas that are in the dryer? And some grape juice from the store? And while you're at it, ice cream? No problem. Grab animal, pj's, ice cream, car keys. Date over.

This is why women, particularly women with children, need to get away. Until you get women away from the house and all its demands, you won't get a woman's full attention.

Many marriage counselors believe that couples should sit down with the calendar in January and plan an overnighter every four to six weeks for the whole year. It sounds unrealistic to many of us, but think about it. If you made it a priority, you *could* find a way to make it happen. People who've taken their marriage counselors' advice swear by it.

The big problem for many of us isn't the *doing it,* it's the *planning it.* And many women first have to get over their guilt about needing to get away. They have to convince themselves first that taking a night away on a regular basis is OK.

Guilt stops many women from going on overnighters or even stealing a few hours for themselves. Women believe they're neglecting their children if they get away once every six weeks. We have a hard time believing that taking care of ourselves is the first and most important step in taking care of the whole family.

If you're a mom, brace yourself for the people who absolutely will not support your getting away regularly. There *will* be judgmental people in your life who might indirectly imply that you're a bad mother because you make getting away as a couple a priority. Unfortunately, it's just the way our culture is. Our society encourages women to put everything else first and ourselves second.

But marriage counselors are very much in agreement on this: what's good for your marriage is good for your children. Whatever you do to strengthen your marriage strengthens the foundation of the whole family. And it's much easier for children to thrive in a happy family. So believe it. You're not being selfish by taking a night away regularly with your spouse. You're quite possibly doing one of the most giving things you could do for your children and your family. It's important.

Sit down with the calendar and plan an overnighter every six weeks for the next six months. See how much better you feel when you take time for romance, your partner, yourself.

> *"[Television] is a medium of entertainment which permits millions of people to listen to the same joke at the same time, and yet remain lonesome."*
> —T.S. Eliot

One romantic challenge our grandparents didn't have was competing with a television in the bedroom for attention. They had maybe one television, and it was in the living or family room.

In our culture, everyone has their own TV and computer, oftentimes sitting in bedrooms like a focal point. We've created armoires and altars to accommodate this magical screen that we worship. And its blankness cries out for pictures, day and night.

A blank TV screen is just too tempting, way too tempting for the bedroom. You're sitting there. He's sitting there. It's sitting there. One of you decides to "just check" to see if anything is on. You get sucked in by a VH1 where-are-they-now documentary about a band you didn't even like when they were popular twenty-five years ago. We get lulled into watching news we don't want to hear, movies we've seen already, sports highlights for games we watched, and inane game shows. Of course, being a news anchor, I'm compelled to say that careless viewing is not such a crime when you've got time to kill, but in the bedroom? No! So many lost opportunities for romance.

Nielsen studies report that Americans watch an average of 3.5 hours of television per day! *Redbook's* online study published in *Redbook's Married Lust* reports that 60 percent of polled couples have sex once a week or less, and 66 percent of couples put the duration of the lovemak-ing at thirty minutes or less. Assuming that the once-a-week or less cou-ples aren't making up for lost time by having marathon sex lasting a full day, we can safely approximate that American couples spend 24.5 hours per week watching television, compared to only a half hour making love!

And there's more. Many studies link TV viewing to insomnia and obe-sity. Remember, romance burns calories, TV viewing does not.

Again, since my primary source of income is through the television, I'd be the last person to suggest you give up TV completely. But it's hard to argue with the evidence that shows that televisions do not belong in the bedroom.

Try it for a month. Put your bedroom TV somewhere else. You may feel withdrawal at first, but with all the romantic advantages, you won't mind them for long. Getting rid of your bedroom television practically guaran-tees that you'll both be in the mood more often.

Loving a Romance Moron

*"Love takes off masks that we fear we cannot live
without and know we cannot live within."*
—James Baldwin

Some men know how to make you weak in the knees just by whispering at that spot on your neck. Some guys know exactly where to make a reservation and how to get that choice table in the corner with the view that's just right for putting you in the mood. But let's be honest. That's not *your* guy.

Your guy adorably bumbles his way through everything. In fact, it's part of the reason why you selected him from all the other fish in the sea. The smooth, suave guys didn't seem sincere to you. You wanted someone who may be clueless, but at least genuine and honorable.

There's a lot to appreciate about romance morons. They often make the best partners for life. Anything they do, they'll do because they mean it, not to worm their way out of trouble or into a fleeting moment of passion. Romance morons are genuinely interested in what will make you happy and more satisfied. This is stuff they really want to know, or *would* want to know if they knew they were missing it. They're the guys who care about when you feel romance is lacking. They care, but they don't know what to *do* about it. And that's where you come in. You'll have to teach them what to do.

A romance moron will not take subtle clues. If you place lit candles around the house, he will dutifully call the power company or check the fuse box. If he walks in the house to find the kids absent, the kitchen smelling fabulous, and you looking ravishing, he'll assume there must be company coming. He'd never guess that all the fuss was for him. He just doesn't get it, but you've got to admit there's something lovable about his humility and unassuming style.

Best of all, romance-challenged men can be taught. They can be trained. But it's not something that's ever going to be second nature to them. So learn to appreciate all their good qualities and learn to create a little romance on your own.

Light candles when you feel like lighting candles. Suggest a moonlit walk when you notice the full moon. Be the first to suggest a little stargazing when you drive out of the city and into the starlit wonder of the country. Make suggestions about overnight dates at nice hotels, and then pick up the phone and hand it to him to emphasize your point. Take the initiative and don't resent having to.

He has a lot of great qualities. Romantic intuitiveness is just not among them. Fortunately, it's not the most important quality for a lifelong partner to have. And also fortunately, he's got you to teach him how to be romantic. You'll probably never find a better student in the world than a good, old-fashioned romance moron. Gotta love 'em.

126.
Standing Appointment for Romance

"The commonest thing is delightful if one only hides it."
—Oscar Wilde

People who are extremely busy and overloaded with responsibilities often have little tricks that help keep them on schedule. People whose jobs require them to ratchet up the frequent flier miles to the same cities over and over again often simplify their lives by taking the same plane, flight number, day, and hour whenever possible. It just cuts down on the number of details they're forced to remember.

I know a lot of people who simplify their schedules by setting their monthly hair appointments for the same day of the same week at the same hour without fail. They never have to make a frantic call to find out when their appointment is. Having regular appointments reduces stress and keeps things orderly. And when others make demands on their time, they always remember *that* block of time is unavailable.

If you're super busy, perhaps the same thing should be done to schedule romantic time with your mate. It could be a half hour once a week, or two hours every other week. Whatever time you set aside for romance with your mate, make it the same exact time, same exact place so that there's no confusion whatsoever.

This is time that's separate from any extra dates you may arrange with your mate. It's time that you have together *no matter what.*

My husband and I have it worked out that when we hear the cartoon music introducing our daughter's favorite television show on the day that my husband always has off, that's our time for love.

When it's scheduled, it's easily remembered and it's also easier to say no to people who are begging for favors. You just tell people that you have a standing appointment at that time. They'll think it's the nail salon or something. Few are so rude as to ask, but if they do, give them the answer! It's your time for romance with your mate. It's much more important than any other demand anyone else could make on your time.

It shouldn't be difficult to convince your mate to commit to the appointment time so long as you find a time that's least likely to be interrupted. It can be 6 A.M. on Thursdays or 11 P.M. on Fridays or any other time that seems best for both your schedules. Just find a time and stick to it.

What to do with that time? Whatever you want. Talk. Make love. Catch up on conversations. Watch a movie. Whatever. Just make it your special time.

Let kids know it's your special time, too. They'll have to work out their own arguments at that time and get their own glass of water. They'll have to struggle through their homework alone for a while. They'll get used to it and they'll reap the benefits to having parents who are close and loving. That's something not many children have these days, and it has a priceless impact on their lives.

I think a once-a-week standing appointment works out best, even if it's only for a half hour. That's still a half hour longer than most couples devote solely to the nourishment of their relationship every week. See what works best for you, but do give a standing appointment a try. You'll like it.

127

Go to Bed Together

*"We find rest in those we love, and we provide a
resting place in ourselves for those who love us."*
—Saint Bernard of Clairvaux

There was a time, not so long ago, when couples were more synchronized. Dinnertime was dinnertime, and bedtime was bedtime. There weren't mealtimes *plural*. There wasn't bedtime for one, and Internet time for the other. There was just bedtime.

Alas, it is very difficult for the modern, dual-career couple to synchronize bedtime. But aren't the romantic advantages of going to bed at the same time obvious? When you're both awake, it's easier to cuddle. It's much harder to cuddle up to someone who's already in the snoring phase.

On the other hand, if you go to bed at the same time, you both start out looking appealing, your breath is still minty fresh, the hour is early, there are no distractions, and the time is ripe for *l'amore!*

One of the typical challenges of setting a bedtime is when one partner is a night owl and the other is an early bird. Compromise is always the key, but it's also probably best if you err on the side of the early bird's schedule.

Being a night owl myself, it's very hard for me to actually give in on this one. But I can't ignore the research, which supports the fact that Americans need to go to bed earlier. (See the "Get More Sleep" chapter for further details.)

Getting to bed earlier and at the same time will give you more time as a couple to read trashy novels aloud to each other, or romantic poetry and letters. You can snuggle to keep each other warm. You can gaze at the moon and stars from your window together, or (gasp!) just talk.

128.
Get More Sleep

"Health is the vital principle of bliss."
—James Thomson

Some of the best holistic medicine experts believe that getting enough sleep is the world's most potent aphrodisiac. It makes sense because when we're rested, we have more energy and are more interested in *everything*, including, and especially, in romance.

But we're a nation of people operating on chronic sleep deprivation. People think it's outrageous if they accidentally sleep for ten hours straight one night, but research shows that getting ten hours of sleep may be exactly what we need *every* night to function at an optimal level. Many of us are walking zombies, operating on an average of six hours of sleep a night. Researchers believe the cumulative effect over a period of time is staggering and dangerous. If romance seems dead sometimes, is it any wonder why?

Dr. James Maas, author of *Power Sleep,* notes that before the invention of the light bulb, people got an average of ten hours of sleep every night.

Can you imagine what your world might look like on ten hours of sleep every night? Is it possible for you to consider that instead of getting *less* done with fewer hours awake, you'd actually get *more* accomplished—and have more time for fun—because you're that much more alert and more competent?

What does all this have to do with romance? Plenty. Once you're getting to bed earlier, you might be amazed at how much more willing you are to consider a little hanky-panky before you turn in.

Try it for a week. Get as close as you can to ten hours sleep every night for one week. You may get hooked, and the whole experience may just take you from "Romance-who?" to "Ooh-la-la!"

129

Get Out of the Rut

*"If your daily life seems poor, do not blame it;
blame yourself, tell yourself that you are not poet
enough to call forth its riches."*
—Rainer Maria Rilke

If you really don't have time for a vacation, and a daring adventure is out of the question, do *something* together to escape the rut.

Leave the house for a few hours together and set out to see a part of town that you've always meant to explore. Make sure it's a place you both want to go, and then set *no* goals. If you only have time to see a tiny bit of this local treasure, fine. You'll hit the rest next time. The only goal you should set is to have fun and not argue, no matter what.

Shake on it. Go out and have a mini adventure! Here are a few easy ideas for breaking the rut:

- Go to a farmer's market and eat fresh fruit.
- Take in an outdoor concert in a genre you don't normally enjoy.
- Take a nature walk and identify plants.
- Go to bed at sundown.
- Eat at an ethnic restaurant you never dared trying before.
- Go to a Little League baseball game, starring no one you know.
- Rent a convertible and drive around, just for fun.
- Take an early morning Tai Chi class together in the park.
- Go snorkeling in your local lake.
- Start a collection together.

• Search out your fantasy neighborhood or summer home.

You're the expert on your particular brand of "rut." You know what you always do. Now go look for opportunities and adventures that you never do. Look through the newspaper "happenings" listings, and try something that you've never done. You only have to do it once to successfully take yourself out of the rut for a day.

130

Minimize Mood-Kill

"I say, when there are spats, kiss and make up before the day is done and live to fight another day."
—Randolph Ray

Every couple has them: sure-fire mood killers. Situations that make romance highly unlikely for the day, and possibly beyond. For some couples, the mood killer is anything to do with home improvement or repairs. It starts with a dreamy vision about home life made better with just one little modification, and the next thing you know they're not speaking to one another and there's a giant hole in the wall. This is a mood killer. I know a few couples who (possibly with the help of antidepressants) see the humor in a gaping-hole-gone-wrong, but the vast majority will suffer romance problems for days, maybe weeks.

In my own relationship, the mood killer is the boat—that damn boat that I practically forced Gary to buy. Maintenance on this tiny ski boat costs a fortune every year, and still, every time we forget what a pain it is and try to take it out on the lake, it doesn't work. There we are, at the boat launch, hundreds of other boaters waiting for their turn to launch, and our newly repaired boat will not start. Not only did this recurring nightmare kill the mood in our marriage, I don't think any single thing we own has brought us closer to calling lawyers and calling it quits.

There are as many mood killers as there are relationships. Some couples do weekly battle over where to eat out. Others have nightly wars over the remote control. While entertaining is a pleasure for some couples, others admit that the stress of throwing a simple, casual party is enough to send their marriage over the edge. Even driving in a car together can end up being a mood-kill experience with effects that last for days.

There are plenty of very serious arguments that kill the romance for a while, and understandably so. But I'm not talking about those arguments. I'm talking about the stupid ones. The boat ones. The hole-in-the-wall ones. The remote-control ones. The arguments that keep romance at bay for no good reason. Those are the ones you've got to eliminate.

Now, relationship researchers and counselors will give you all kinds of conflicting advice on how to deal with conflict. But one common theme is this: learn how to avoid the overheated argument without avoiding the partner.

Here's an example: I want to have a romantic evening with my husband. He suggests a moonlit ride on the boat. I say great, but while I'm making the food, he'll need to take the boat, perhaps with the help of a friend, and get it into the water at the boat launch. We're still going to have our romantic evening, but I'm just not going to be there during that hour or so when the boat, as always, refuses to start. I'll make sure to have wine chilled and ready to cool his temper as he tells me all about the latest boat frustrations. All I'm doing is avoiding the situation that's a sure-fire mood killer. I'm not avoiding him.

For the couple who constantly argues over where to eat out, the answer is not in skipping dinner, but offering to give him his choice this time and promising to take your turn next time. Not avoiding each other, just the mood killer.

Ever notice how ritual battles are scripted and practically choreographed so that they happen the same way, pushing the same buttons every time? We just have to break free from those ritual arguments and look at them in a fresh light. Avoid the problem, not the partner.

131.

Celebrate Birthdays
Six Times a Year

"Human felicity is produced not so much by great pieces of good fortune that seldom happen as by little advantages that occur every day."

—Benjamin Franklin

It's not that I want to get older six times faster, and I certainly don't need gifts lavished on me multiple times a year. But I think it's criminal that we each only get one day a year when we get everything exactly the way we want it: go to the restaurant of our choice, see the movie that we want to see with no compromising for anyone else's taste. It's easily accepted that your birthday is *your* day to do whatever and go wherever you wish. It just doesn't seem right that we're only treated to a day like that but once a year.

That's why I recommend that each person get six days a year to be totally selfish and uncompromising. For couples, that would mean that it's one or the other's birthday for one day every month. No need for any extravagant birthday accoutrements, just dates when one person can, without apology, without guilt, get to do exactly what he/she wants.

Birthdays are the only days in the year when we don't demand compromise and consideration for the other person's wishes. On all the rest of your dates, where you go and what you do is tactfully negotiated like a resolution before the United Nations Security Council. Wouldn't it be great, six times a year, to be able to get your own way without hesitation or negotiation? Think how happy he'd be to be able to dine out, without guilt or pleading, at a sports bar with nineteen big-screen televisions surrounding you, blasting out the games, highlights, and slow-motion replays. On his birthday, you're happy to give him that one special night where he's free to choose the most tasteless, annoying restaurant he can find. Is it fair that he only gets that night once a year?

Is it fair that you only get to eat at the restaurant that has dim lighting, soft music, and *no* eighteen-ounce portions of red meat on the menu only once a year? Heck no! Claim your birthday rights six times a year each, and happily indulge in the night of his choice, knowing that your night is coming up just one month down the road.

Let him request you wear that dress he loves on *his* special night. Ask him to wear a tie on *your* night. Be demanding about the romance you're looking for in the same way you would on your birthday, or—why not?— get even more brazen in your romantic demands. Tell him he's your love-slave for the night and demand complete obedience and satisfaction!

132

Let Others Be Your Worst Critics

"We find fault with perfection itself."
—Blaise Pascal

You'll be amazed by how much more romantic your relationship can be once you decide to let others be your worst critics. Nobody needs another critic in his life. The world, it seems, tries to beat us down into submission. "You're too fat," we see and hear in the media. "You're not executive material," we may hear at work.

We're constantly criticized everywhere we go in some form or another. Some of us are more sensitive to it than others, but eventually it gets us all down. Everywhere we turn we're reminded that we don't measure up to society's image of perfection, which is unattainable even for those who seem to have it all.

You can enhance the romance in your life and help yourself feel more romantic if you make a pact to let others be your worst critics. Promise to each other that within the walls of your home and the comfort of your relationship, you will help create a safe, warm place—free from criticism. It's another way you can be nurturing to each other. As the world tries to tear you down, use your relationship to build each other back up.

A promise not to be critical is an easy one to make and a very hard one to keep. My husband, however, is the master at it. Everything I know about being supportive, I learned through his being so kind and gentle with me.

Since my husband and I are in the same vicious business (TV news) I used to offer my husband constructive criticism. "You really should wear that longer beige jacket, not the one with the gathered waist. Gathers emphasize the waistline," I'd tell him, thinking I'd cleverly and diplomatically avoided any hint of implication that he had a spare tire around his waist. "I liked the way you said that the council failed to pinpoint the exact cost, but I really think you should have said *that* part in front of the vacant lot," I'd *helpfully* suggest. He would smile and seem to listen, but rarely responded. And he *never* offered a critique of me to return the favor.

One day I asked him why he never gave me constructive criticism. He said he knew that dozens of people criticized me daily. This is true. As a news anchor, there isn't a day that goes by that I don't have people telling me that my hair doesn't look right, I made a grammatical error, or I must be having an "off" night. I've even had rumors start that I was pregnant when I wasn't. Just *try* to convince yourself that people don't think you're fat or looking unusually pudgy when a rumor like that starts going around.

Gary told me he never wanted to be lumped in with my "critics." I had enough of those. He said he just wanted to be there to love and support me.

What a wise, good man. I immediately stopped critiquing him and started doing a better job of supporting him. I still slip once in a while, but I *try* a lot harder now.

It's another change that's revived the romance in our marriage, making us feel adored and safe together.

133

Vacation Apart

*"Absence lessens ordinary passions and augments
great ones, as the wind blows out a candle
and makes a fire blaze."*
—François Duc de la Rochefoucauld

V acations are supposed to be a time to catch up on romance; that's why it's important to vacation apart. Not *completely* apart, just for several hours every day.

This advice obviously doesn't apply to the lucky few couples I know who love to do all the same things all the time. If both of you can't get enough of white-water rafting, vacation planning is easy. The rest of us have it tougher.

Many otherwise happy couples can't agree on what to do on a vacation. While this may sound stereotypical, a lot of women (like me) love to shop. A lot of men (like my husband) would rather endure anything than get wrangled into shopping while on vacation.

While togetherness sounds great, too much of it can be a very bad thing for romance. Agreeing on a common activity leads to arguments, arguments lead us away from romance. After all, most of us lead pretty independent lives when *not* on vacation. You do your thing, he does his thing, for at least eight hours a day. Then you meet up for dinner and the remains of the day. It's a system that works well, and works even better while on vacation.

That's why the best places to vacation are places where there's something for everyone, and no pressure to be together all the time. Do your own thing by day, make mad passionate romance by night. It's amazing how a little time apart can lead to better romance.

It took one horrible European vacation for me to learn this bit of vacation wisdom. It was supposed to be the romantic trip of a lifetime—Paris, the French Riviera, Portofino, Italy. How could it fail? Easily, that's how.

We stuck together like glue, and that was our mistake. While I wanted to hit all the sights and museums, he desperately wanted to see the *uncharted* Europe. Being the rugged, outdoorsy type, he somehow had it in his mind that we were going hiking through Europe. I was really having a hard time picturing myself passing up the Louvre to go in search of some wilderness hiking experience in PARIS! I protested, he gave in and toured the tourist sights and was miserable. I was too. We needed relaxation and romance; we got neither.

We later wondered why we'd been so determined to stick together every hour of every day of the trip, when we were clearly interested in doing different things. I guess we thought we *had* to be together, that that was the whole point of the vacation. But it really wasn't.

As we tried to figure out the secret to a successful romantic vacation together, we remembered another romantic trip that really *was* romantic.

We honeymooned in breathtaking Banff, Canada. Knowing Gary liked to ski and I didn't, we planned on spending time apart. By day, he'd be skiing, hiking, and wandering. I'd be spa-ing, shopping, and reading. Then we'd dress up and go to dinner together, every night like our wedding night, perfect and romantic. It was the best trip of our lives.

Evaluating the trips we'd taken, my husband and I realized that in order for vacations to be romantic, they also have to help each individual relax, unwind, and rejuvenate the spirit. Each person does that in their own way.

Gary needs to hike and be physical. I need to pamper myself and be very still. If we take care of our own spiritual needs, fill up reserves that have gone dry, we soon find we're ready for romance.

It's a hard-learned lesson that I should have picked up from my parents, married happily for thirty-six years. Not only do they do their own thing while on vacation together, they often vacation apart. They come back home to each other with more love to offer.

But you don't have to isolate yourself for weeks to get the same bene-fits. Just loosen the grip on your time demands. Vacation like honey-mooners. Relax and trust that the romance will be there, even if you spend daytime hours apart. It still leaves the whole night for sweet, sweet love.

134.

Sing His Praises

"The deafest man can hear praise, and is slow to think any an excess."
—Walter Savage Landor

It's easy to see the worst in people. It's much harder to live with someone day in and day out and keep focusing on their best qualities. Seeing the best in your mate is one of the keys to keeping romance alive and thriving.

It's a talent my friend Sally has, and I really admire it. While all the rest of the wives and girlfriends are caught up in a group griping session about how selfish and awful our mates are, she focuses on the positive. She sees the best in her husband. It's a talent not limited to newlyweds—Sally has been married for fifteen years.

I have never, ever heard Sally say something negative about her husband's character. She'll take small, humorous jabs in front of her husband about his not helping at all with the neighborhood garage sale, or not getting a project done that he planned on doing years ago. She'll smile and tell you he's not perfect. But if you wait for her to point out serious character flaws in her husband, flaws that she seems distressed over or can't find a lot of humor in—you'll be waiting a long time. Sally knows she's got a good thing, and she focuses on her husband's best qualities.

Sally's husband Larry is just as kind and generous. He lifts her up, never brings her down. I can't imagine his ever saying anything really unkind about her. He's a gentle soul, and they share a gentle and loving relationship.

What's the end result of all this positivity and commitment to focusing on each other's best qualities? A relationship that has a lot of warmth, a lot of closeness. A relationship that's free from many of the obstacles that other couples construct.

When we're critical, when we focus on the bad instead of the good, our partners resent it and start looking for the worst in us. We start building walls between us that end up being propped up for years (maybe forever) by a constant flow of hurt feelings on both sides of the wall.

We *all* have bad qualities. The fastest way to get your partner to find *yours* is to focus on *his*. It's the ugly side of relationships and it isn't necessary. When it comes right down to it, we can never really change people anyway, so focusing on flaws is pointless. Publicly celebrate your mate's good qualities and you'll build a warm relationship that's ripe for romance and will last forever.

135.

Embrace "Good Enough"

"Perfection has one grave defect: it is apt to be dull."
—W. Somerset Maugham

Years ago, I did the unthinkable while giving a speech to a club for mothers in Portland, Oregon. I spoke out against Martha Stewart when she was enjoying the height of her popularity and women everywhere where trying to figure out how they too could be a little more like Martha.

At the time, she seemed to have quite a lot, if not everything. She had a thriving business and successful men standing in line to escort her to her latest VIP engagement. We knew she had a daughter and several homes and she was able to do what none of the rest of us could manage: everything. She knew how to get back that perfect, untarnished gleam to copper cookware. She knew how to make a soufflé and maintain a perfect five-acre garden. Her homes were spotless and impeccably organized and somehow she managed to run her billion-dollar business brilliantly, too. We all knew, deep down in our hearts, that doing all this was really impossible, but many of us had just convinced ourselves (quite easily, actually) that the only reason why we couldn't do the same as Martha is that we were simply inadequate. We weren't trying hard enough, or weren't focused enough or just weren't good enough. Maybe if we just tried harder, we could one day do it all like Martha.

That day at the mothers' tea, I spoke out. I couldn't stand it anymore. I was no more of an expert than anyone else there, but I had a career on

TV, so they thought I must have *something* to say to give their tea meaning that day. I had free reign and I decided to finally say something about this insane perfection we were all striving for.

"Let's get our priorities straight. We can't do it all, and we'll never be able to do it all."

It was a pretty bold speech back then. I was sick of feeling inadequate, and I was hoping someone else was too. I didn't get much of a response that day, but only a few months later, kicking Martha Stewart became a national pastime. While we all still loved watching her show and bought her products (me too), everyone finally conceded that aiming for Martha-like perfection was ridiculous.

What does all this have to do with love and romance? Everything, in my book (and it *is* my book). Worrying about the gleam of my copper cookware, on top of all my other responsibilities, I had less time to cuddle with my husband on the couch. Designing a rotating spice rack for my fresh herbs from my kitchen-garden was not only a full-time job, it wasn't as much fun as going to see a movie with Gary. I learned that with all my unavoidable daily responsibilities, I really don't have very much time for any other lofty domestic goals if I'm going to have any time for the one thing that is truly the most important thing in my house: my marriage.

I had to learn to embrace "good enough." In order to have time for my children and the love of my life, it has to be OK that my house doesn't look like the pictures in a magazine.

I'll admit that striving for *imperfection* for the sake of deeper loving has not always been easy. There are days when I find myself totally obsessed or depressed about the state of my imperfect domicile. But choices have to be made in a twenty-four-hour day.

My living room will never end up in *Better Homes and Gardens*, but it's good enough that it's cozy for movie night, Gary and me cuddled under a blanket, fireplace blazing.

Today, embrace good enough and choose love over laundry. Where is your mate right now? Go and do a little smooching.

136

Romance, Unplugged

"Many a time the thing left silent makes for happiness."
—Pindar

We're all too accessible these days. It's almost unthinkable that someone should *not* be able to reach you. Either you're available by land line or cell phone. If your cell phone is busy, someone might try your pager or your email. In a pinch, they'll even call your neighbor on *her* cell phone and ask her to go over to your house and ask you to turn your cell phone back on. Aaargh! It's enough to drive you mad.

God forbid you should actually not be available for an hour or so. People might think you've fallen off the ends of the Earth.

Have you noticed that everything these days is *urgent?* It's not just a phone call from a client who needs help, it's an *urgent* phone call from a client who *urgently* needs help. Sound familiar?

For the sake of resurrecting a little romance and time to be creative in your life, think about the *unthinkable. Unplug* regularly. If you should be lucky enough to find a time when you and your mate are able to have a quiet lunch at home one day, unplug the phones. Turn off your pagers. Turn off your cell phones. Turn off the computer, lock the door, and let the whole world assume you've either died or had some massive telecommunications meltdown.

The only way to find a little time for romance these days is to seize it and put a stranglehold on it with the promise that you'll kill or die for it. I am being very dramatic here, but so is everyone else these days. Everyone is so dramatic about their need for your time and energy. The only way you'll ever get a little of it for yourself is to be equally dramatic. Turn off your phones without apology. If someone later asks why you were unreachable, tell them you were making love to your husband. That ought to shut them up.

Reclaim your life and your chances for romance. Just unplug regularly. Tell people you unplug frequently so that you can have a whole uninterrupted conversation with your sweetheart. You'll get stares of disbelief, but don't waver. Just unplug.

137.

Mood and the Brood

"There is no slave out of heaven like a loving woman; and, of all loving women, there is no such slave as a mother."
—Henry Ward Beecher

One of the toughest times in a woman's life to feel romantic is just after childbirth and while she's still nursing. Fortunately, feel-good hormones kick in to make life tolerable. But still, at the end of the day, with the baby asleep (temporarily), romance, or touching of any kind, is just about the last thing on Mommy's mind.

She feels tugged at and pulled on all day long. She's discovered the actual purpose for her breasts. And while it's a beautiful experience overall, one that most women wouldn't give up for anything, it's draining. It makes a woman wish for just a few hours of adult conversation, with no one attached to her or pulling at her.

Dads, active parents though they are these days, still get left out during the nursing stage. Not only are they treated like second-class citizens by the baby (who only wants the parent with milk), they also get shoved aside by their wives, who demand sleep and NO MORE GROPING! Its amazing that any relationship survives this phase.

Going on dates together as soon as possible can be a saving grace. But how can you have a romantic date when one person feels totally neglected and the other person is going to scream if she experiences her spouse tugging at her body? Give touch-free dating a try.

It's not that a woman with small children doesn't *ever* want to be touched by her mate. It's just that she doesn't want to be pawed.

Explain to your mate that you look forward to having a wonderful, romantic physical experience with him. But for the first two hours of a date, you just need to unwind and not feel the tug of any kind of touching. If your mate understands that this is completely normal, that 90 percent of the other women with babies feel exactly the same way, he's less likely to take it personally and perceive it as your rejecting him physically.

Two hours of touch-free dating is all you need to make yourself right. Of course, if you head back home right after those two hours, you'll come home to chaos and a baby demanding to be allowed to touch and grope a lot more. So don't go home right away. Find a place outside your home to have a romantic moment. If you have a minivan, this is no problem (and you thought minivans were just for carpools!). Go see a drive-in movie, or head to "lover's lane." This is also an excellent time to check the home of a friend you're house-sitting for (do they have a make-out couch?). As a last resort, you could get a cheapish hotel room for an hour. Since you've now had two hours of no touching, your body and mind will be much more open to physical romance.

Moms can feel the stress of being overly needed at many points in their lives, even after the babies are well on their way to being young adults. Dads feel the strain, too. Vow to each other that as you both raise the brood, you'll be sensitive to each other's needs and feelings. You'll try to give each other space when you need it, and closeness too. Promise that you won't become automatically defensive or hurt if *he says* he needs two hours of silence, or *you say* you need two hours of physical distance. Its not personal, just a need that longs to be filled before anything else can take place.

Before becoming a mom, I never dreamed that I would one day dream of two hours of touch-free existence and see it as perfect romantic paradise. Gary never dreamed that getting a few hours of uninterrupted sleep would be the stuff of fantasy.

Being parents together is tough—wonderful, but tough. There's still room for romance, if you help each other meet some basic needs: sleep, sanity, and a little separation once in a while.

138

According to Stan

*"History is bright and fiction dull with homely men
who have charmed women."*
—O. Henry

Stan is just another ordinary guy I know, except one thing: he's brilliant when it comes to romancing his wife.

Stan and I used to work in the same office, and his wife was the envy of every woman there. Stan is not fantastic looking. He's not rich, he's not particularly tall, and he doesn't seem to be much of a smooth talker. But Stan treats his wife like a queen and all the women in the office sat in awe listening to the stories of the latest sweet thing he'd done for his wife. Like spending a lot of time picking out the perfect Coach briefcase (guaranteed to last forever) for her when she got a promotion. What a guy.

Stan is the kind of guy who'll stroll into an uptown store and buy his wife a beautiful dress he saw in the window for no special reason except that he thought it would look stunning on her. He has taste. He has sensitivity. He has three older sisters.

That was the big secret of Stan's romantic success, by his own admission. "Growing up with three sisters, you hear *everything*. You learn everything about what a woman wants, what hurts her feelings, and what makes her feel better," he'd tell us office women swarming around his desk. We sat with gaping mouths as he described how he wooed his pretty wife. *Wooed!* You could actually use the word *woo* to describe how he courted (yes, courted!) his wife.

Stan knows women. He knows all about periods and feeling overly emotional (but defensive about anyone even suggesting *that's* the reason), he knows about bloating, and how it feels when a man stands you up. Stan knows how to listen to a woman complain about the same problem for thirty-seven minutes without once interrupting to offer a solution.

Stan never has trouble finding his wife a wonderfully expensive gift for a special occasion, but understands that the best gifts aren't necessarily expensive and are for no special occasion at all. Stan knows how to make dinner reservations someplace special, and he knows where his wife keeps the names and phone numbers for the baby-sitters. He likes surprising her with a special evening out.

Everything Stan knows about women he attributes to being the only son in a house full of women. Stan taught me something very important about romance and understanding women: it's taught and it's learned.

Stan did not come into this world with a special intuitiveness about women. He's not an especially intuitive guy. He's not feminine. He's not an avid shopper or one of those guys who only hangs out around women. He likes sports. I think he hates shopping malls as much as the next guy. All he knows about romance he learned from the women in his life.

The moral of this story is, if you're single, you must select from your prospects a man with three older sisters. For the married woman, the moral is that even sisterless men will need to be taught to understand us. They *can* be taught. They *must* be taught. And we must be patient.

Remember, you're training a man and that requires patience. As Rebecca Rosenblat (a.k.a. "Dr. Date") tells me, "Women need to show men the same kind of softness and patience that they show their children." I asked her if that wasn't a little insulting to men. She said no, explaining that we usually hold our men up to impossible expectations.

"You're teaching them things for the first time. Give your man the same kindness and gentleness that you'd give anyone else in your life that you care deeply for."

Wise words and good advice. Whenever I have a tough time following that advice, I think of Stan. Stan is the goal and Gary is inching toward him (sometimes at an agonizingly slow pace, I'll admit) every day. But he's getting there, and I love him for being so willing to learn.

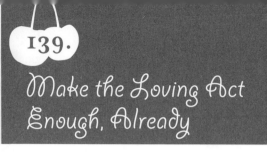

139

Make the Loving Act Enough, Already

> *"In order to love simply, it is necessary to know how to show love."*
>
> —Fyodor Dostoevsky

y uncle tells a great story about his first love. She was a churchgoer; he wasn't. In spite of their religious differences, the young couple was very much in love and looked to be heading down the aisle.

One day, their differences came to a head.

"I want you to go to church. It's important to me that you go regularly," she said.

"OK, if it's important to you, I will go," he answered.

"But do you *want* to go?" she asked.

"No, I don't want to go. But I do want you to be happy, so if it will make you happy and it's important to you, I will go," said my uncle.

"That's not enough," she insisted. "You have to *want* to go. You can't just go because I'm asking you to go to church, you have to *want* to go."

"Well, now you're asking me for something that I can't give you," answered my uncle.

Before long, the young lovers tearfully went their separate ways.

I can't help but think how shortsighted it was of my uncle's girlfriend to give up on him so easily. Just agreeing to *go* to church was a pretty big step for him, and who knows where it would have led him spiritually? Maybe eventually he'd be going to church, not just for her, but because he was really getting something out of it. Those things happen over time and through experience.

The story also makes me think about how often we, as women, make this same kind of mistake with our otherwise-willing men. We want them to share their feelings and it's not enough that they *do;* we further insist that they *want* to spill their emotions and even enjoy the experience. It's not enough for us that we train them to light candles and sprinkle rose petals on the bed sheets—we demand that they *understand* why it's so important to be so romantic, and we expect that they should not only go along with it, but embrace it wholeheartedly. Why isn't it enough for us that we just get them to be romantic, for whatever reason or motivation?

They won't be yearning for candlelight. Holding hands is something they'll do because it's important to *us,* not necessarily to them. Kissing in the moonlight or rocking on the porch will be something they'll do to make us happy and because we'll be grateful and maybe more willing to be intimate.

The bottom line is, if our men are listening to our needs and trying to fulfill them, we should allow that to be enough. Maybe someday, they too will *want* the candlelight. Maybe after a thousand long talks he participates in just to make you happy, he'll feel the comfort and pleasure of connecting that way and will *want* to talk more often. But if that never happens, it's still pretty great that he cares enough about you to give you what you need, even though he's really not into it.

Consider letting your needs live independently from his desires. How freeing and wonderful it is to get roses and candlelight without worrying about whether it lights his fire, too. Heaps of gratitude for a loving act will guarantee that you get more of what it is that you want, and the gratitude may—more than anything else—make your mate enjoy making your romantic dreams come true.

140.

Make Expectations Clear

"Venus favors the bold."
—Ovid

Polls indicate that about half of all men *dread* Valentine's Day. They know that something big is expected of them, but they have no idea what it is and how to make it happen. They'd like to do something creative and romantic, but when they draw a blank, they end up at the flower shop.

Take pity on your poor Romeo and tell him *months* in advance what your Valentine's/birthday/anniversary expectations are. He may be relieved to know that all you're really looking for is a candlelit dinner in a cozy restaurant, maybe a single rose, and his full attention.

If it's a surprise you're really after, allow the choice of restaurant to be enough of a surprise. If your man is anything like mine, he will need to be informed that reservations on Valentine's Day are hard to come by, so plan on making them three months in advance.

Give him the joy of being a hero. Get clear on your own desires for these romantic days, and talk about it. Give him hints. Clip out ads for romantic restaurants and sneak them into his wallet or planner.

Once you've made your desires for a romantic day clear, sit back and relax. If you get a bouquet of flowers, appreciate it. Heavy praising is the surest way to get more and better romance the next time around. Rome wasn't built in a day, and neither are romantic men. They learn through communication, hints, and *tons* of praise.

141.

Banish "The Way We Were"

"In memory everything seems to happen to music."
—Tennessee Williams

It's hard to let go of the past, the way we used to be. As a relationship grows and changes, we often struggle to try to get back to "the way we were."

But a relationship has to evolve to survive; we can't stay the same and we can't go backward.

It's something to think about as you try to recapture romance. Don't try to re-create the romance of the past; try to create a new romance for a new future together.

Change is scary. It's natural to feel terrified as you become more independent, autonomous but still connected in just the right way. Relationship researchers say that as a relationship develops, two people gradually end the illusion that they are one person and start to grow apart, creating a new, more mature picture of a relationship where the two are separate individuals but still connected in key ways. It's like growing into the monogrammed towels that say "his," "hers," and "ours."

Most divorces happen while couples are in that transition from being joined-at-the hip to having some autonomy but still trying to remain a couple. Each person (often at different times) resists the change. But the change is absolutely normal and necessary. Embracing the transition is the challenge.

It's during those transitional years that couples could most benefit from a little outside help, a marriage or couples' counselor.

You can also learn a lot from books written by brilliant researchers on successful marriages, such as *The Seven Principles for Making Marriage Work* by John Gottman, Ph.D.

At the heart of what brought you together, there remains, through all the changes, something special that can keep you together. The secret to success may be not clinging so tightly to the memories of the past, but looking with anticipation to the future and what can still be wonderful about your relationship.

To keep your focus on the future, regularly bring up hopes and dreams for the future. Ask him about his dreams. Share yours. Not just the dreams about you as a couple, but dreams about your family, your career, your spirituality—all the things that round out your wonderful life.

By sharing together, we make each other a partner, a coconspirator in those dreams, even if our dreams are completely different. There is a place in the middle where the "us" can still live, breathe, and flourish.

Memories of the first days of love, like wedding photos, are wonderful to look back on and cherish. As I look back at those photos, I see romance and love, but I also see wide-eyed innocence and naiveté. As I look at photos of us now, I see two people who have a better idea of the challenges ahead, two people more creative about keeping romance alive. I see two people who could do it alone, but choose to walk through life hand in hand. We're better together now than we were then, and we'll be better still tomorrow.

142

It's the Little Things

"Men trip not on mountains, they stumble on stones."
—Hindustani proverb

There's a phrase we hear a lot: "Take care of the big things, and the little things will take care of themselves." But for love and romance, just the opposite is true. We have to take care of the little things if we want the big things to go right.

It's the little things like hugging often, kissing at least a few times a day, telling each other to have a good day and then asking about it at the end of the day that really matter. It's little things like saying thank you, saying you're sorry, praising someone for a job well done, and taking the time to really listen.

When you take care of the little things, you take care of some of the big things like closeness, intimacy, and feeling loved automatically. Of course, those little things need to be given and received. You can't take care of the little things for *both of you*. But I've found that if you ask for an inch and then give a mile yourself, it's not long before a true love is happy to meet you halfway.

Take care of the little things, and the big things will take care of themselves. Most people would include fidelity among the big things. There are a lot of reasons for infidelity, and we all know that sex is only one of them.

It's common to hear people who cheat talk about lots of little needs being fulfilled besides just sex:

"She listens to me. She thinks I'm an exciting, attractive guy!"

"He sees me as more than just a housekeeper and baby-sitter. He touches me like my husband used to."

It never ceases to surprise me how little sex or novelty has to do with infidelity. For many people, it's not novelty at all that they're looking for, but rather familiarity, the old familiar way that their spouses *used to* look at them, listen to them, touch them.

Drifting apart is another one of the biggies. But it's pretty hard to drift apart when you're taking a few minutes every day to communicate, be supportive, and touch each other in a way that says *I love you; I'm still here for you.*

Take the time today to work on another little thing or two, and you'll find the whole energy of a relationship starting to change for the better.

section nine

afterglow

143

The End, the Beginning

*"A journey of a thousand miles must begin
with a single step."*
—Chinese proverb

I started working on this book with one premise guiding me: that women are by nature romantic, sensual beings. But in the course of our lives, things happen that move us slowly away from that primal, natural side of our being. One day, we wake up and it's just not there anymore, or it is so faint that getting it back seems hopeless.

I looked around me and saw women just like me, women with a romantic, spiritual side that had shut down. I saw that I and many other women around me were starving. Romantically, spiritually, sensually starving. As we starved, our relationships suffered too; our families and children suffered because we weren't taking care of ourselves and our needs for authenticity.

But in that hopelessness, I also saw a glimmer of what could be. Women loving their bodies, nurturing their sensuality, respecting their needs for romantic expression, and I saw that with just the tiniest shift in thinking, a whole life, a whole family could change for the better. A wilted flower could be brought back to life just by giving it the water and sunlight that it needs.

I started exploring ideas and talking to women, hearing what they had to say about romance and their sensuality; what made them feel "in the mood" and why they thought they were in the mood so rarely. I listened to people who dedicate their lives to helping women reconnect with their romantic nature and helping couples get back on the right track, and I talked to couples who never lost their way to learn their secrets.

Thankfully, I discovered that what we can do to bring back the romance in our lives isn't really hard work at all—it's fun. Changing one tiny thing in your day, doing one thing that expresses your romantic nature or celebrates your love of life and your partner, can change the whole world.

Being honest with your partner and bringing him in will change your life. Taking responsibility for the romance you want to experience every day of your life can transform it almost instantly. It's more of a shift in thinking than a stack of new projects to undertake.

The ideas I mentioned in this book were designed to get you to think out of the box and help you to rediscover your own romantic nature. Some of the ideas you'll never try, but maybe they'll inspire you to come up with ideas of your own. Try new things. Be playful, be loving, be sexy, be romantic, be the nurturer, and pamper yourself, too.

The most important thing is to be true to yourself and honor your feminine nature. Feel the transformation in your life and your relationships as you become more romantically *you*.

About the Author

Cam Johnson is the primetime television interviewer for Northwest Cable News, a twenty-four hour news station broadcast throughout the northwestern United States. She anchored the news at stations in Texas and Oregon before coming back home to the Seattle area. She lives on Seattle's east side with her husband, who is a television reporter, and their two young children. *Eat Chocolate Naked* is her first book.